W9-DHU-904

OPPOSING
VIEWPOINTS®
SERIES

American Values

Other Books of Related Interest:

Opposing Viewpoints Series

America's Global Influence

Human Rights

Voting Rights

At Issue Series

How Safe Is America's Infrastructure?

National Security

Current Controversies Series

Globalization

Homeland Security

"Congress shall make no law . . . abridging the freedom of speech, or of the press."

First Amendment to the U.S. Constitution

The basic foundation of our democracy is the First Amendment guarantee of freedom of expression. The Opposing Viewpoints Series is dedicated to the concept of this basic freedom and the idea that it is more important to practice it than to enshrine it.

OPPOSING
VIEWPOINTS®
SERIES

American Values

David M. Haugen, Book Editor

GREENHAVEN PRESS
A part of Gale, Cengage Learning

GALE
CENGAGE Learning

Detroit • New York • San Francisco • New Haven, Conn • Waterville, Maine • London

_# 192079 797_

Christine Nasso, *Publisher*
Elizabeth Des Chenes, *Managing Editor*

© 2009 Greenhaven Press, a part of Gale, Cengage Learning.

Gale and Greenhaven Press are registered trademarks used herein under license.

For more information, contact:
Greenhaven Press
27500 Drake Rd.
Farmington Hills, MI 48331-3535
Or you can visit our Internet site at gale.cengage.com

For product information and technology assistance, contact us at

Gale Customer Support, 1-800-877-4253
For permission to use material from this text or product, submit all requests online at
www.cengage.com/permissions

Further permissions questions can be emailed to permissionrequest@cengage.com

Articles in Greenhaven Press anthologies are often edited for length to meet page requirements. In addition, original titles of these works are changed to clearly present the main thesis and to explicitly indicate the author's opinion. Every effort is made to ensure that Greenhaven Press accurately reflects the original intent of the authors. Every effort has been made to trace the owners of copyrighted material.

Cover photograph reproduced by permission of Image Studios/Getty Images.

LIBRARY OF CONGRESS CATALOGING-IN-PUBLICATION DATA

American Values / David M. Haugen, book editor.
    p. cm. -- (Opposing viewpoints)
    Includes bibliographical references and index.
    ISBN-13: 978-0-7377-4190-2 (hardcover)
    ISBN-13: 978-0-7377-4191-9 (pbk.)
    Social values--United States. I. Haugen, David M., 1969-
    HN90.M6A445 2009
    303.3'720973--dc22

                                                                    2008031771

Contents

Chapter 3: How Should Patriotism Be Defined?

Chapter 4: Can American Values Bridge Cultural Divides?

Why Consider Opposing Viewpoints?

> *"The only way in which a human being can make some approach to knowing the whole of a subject is by hearing what can be said about it by persons of every variety of opinion and studying all modes in which it can be looked at by every character of mind. No wise man ever acquired his wisdom in any mode but this."*
>
> John Stuart Mill

In our media-intensive culture it is not difficult to find differing opinions. Thousands of newspapers and magazines and dozens of radio and television talk shows resound with differing points of view. The difficulty lies in deciding which opinion to agree with and which "experts" seem the most credible. The more inundated we become with differing opinions and claims, the more essential it is to hone critical reading and thinking skills to evaluate these ideas. Opposing Viewpoints books address this problem directly by presenting stimulating debates that can be used to enhance and teach these skills. The varied opinions contained in each book examine many different aspects of a single issue. While examining these conveniently edited opposing views, readers can develop critical thinking skills such as the ability to compare and contrast authors' credibility, facts, argumentation styles, use of persuasive techniques, and other stylistic tools. In short, the Opposing Viewpoints Series is an ideal way to attain the higher-level thinking and reading skills so essential in a culture of diverse and contradictory opinions.

In addition to providing a tool for critical thinking, Opposing Viewpoints books challenge readers to question their own strongly held opinions and assumptions. Most people form their opinions on the basis of upbringing, peer pressure, and personal, cultural, or professional bias. By reading carefully balanced opposing views, readers must directly confront new ideas as well as the opinions of those with whom they disagree. This is not to simplistically argue that everyone who reads opposing views will—or should—change his or her opinion. Instead, the series enhances readers' understanding of their own views by encouraging confrontation with opposing ideas. Careful examination of others' views can lead to the readers' understanding of the logical inconsistencies in their own opinions, perspective on why they hold an opinion, and the consideration of the possibility that their opinion requires further evaluation.

Evaluating Other Opinions

To ensure that this type of examination occurs, Opposing Viewpoints books present all types of opinions. Prominent spokespeople on different sides of each issue as well as well-known professionals from many disciplines challenge the reader. An additional goal of the series is to provide a forum for other, less known, or even unpopular viewpoints. The opinion of an ordinary person who has had to make the decision to cut off life support from a terminally ill relative, for example, may be just as valuable and provide just as much insight as a medical ethicist's professional opinion. The editors have two additional purposes in including these less known views. One, the editors encourage readers to respect others' opinions—even when not enhanced by professional credibility. It is only by reading or listening to and objectively evaluating others' ideas that one can determine whether they are worthy of consideration. Two, the inclusion of such viewpoints encourages the important critical thinking skill of objectively evaluating an author's credentials and bias. This evaluation will illuminate an author's reasons for taking a particular stance on an issue and will aid in readers' evaluation of the author's ideas.

It is our hope that these books will give readers a deeper understanding of the issues debated and an appreciation of the complexity of even seemingly simple issues when good and honest people disagree. This awareness is particularly important in a democratic society such as ours in which people enter into public debate to determine the common good. Those with whom one disagrees should not be regarded as enemies but rather as people whose views deserve careful examination and may shed light on one's own.

Thomas Jefferson once said that "difference of opinion leads to inquiry, and inquiry to truth." Jefferson, a broadly educated man, argued that "if a nation expects to be ignorant and free . . . it expects what never was and never will be." As individuals and as a nation, it is imperative that we consider the opinions of others and examine them with skill and discernment. The Opposing Viewpoints Series is intended to help readers achieve this goal.

David L. Bender and Bruno Leone,
Founders

Introduction

> "America is great because she is good. If America ceases to be good, America will cease to be great."
>
> A remark attributed to
> Alexis de Tocqueville and
> quoted by several U.S. presidents
> and other politicians

> "America is a great force for freedom and prosperity. Yet our greatness is not measured in power or luxuries, but by who we are and how we treat one another. So we strive to be a compassionate, decent, hopeful society."
>
> President George W. Bush,
> 2006 State of the Union Address

British wit and social critic G.K. Chesterton once asserted, "America is the only nation in the world that is founded on a creed. That creed is set forth with dogmatic and even theological lucidity in the Declaration of Independence." The creed Chesterton spoke of during his tour of America in 1921 is that which Thomas Jefferson enshrined in the national memory when he drafted the Declaration of Independence. "We hold these truths to be self-evident," Jefferson stated, "that all men are created equal, that they are endowed by their Creator with certain unalienable Rights, that among these are Life, Liberty, and the Pursuit of Happiness." While both Chesterton and Jefferson acknowledged the religious dimension of these assumed rights, Americans have often focused on the unique and unalienable nature of their creed rather than on the grace of its endowment. All Americans, then, share in a fundamental belief that the virtues of life, liberty, and happiness should be available to all and cannot be revoked without destroying the principles that set America apart from other nations.

It may be indefensible to suggest that America has always lived up to its creed, but it is less controversial to argue that the country has always professed its intention to live by values that stem from Jefferson's self-evident truths. The adherence to such unifying values struck visitors like Chesterton as extraordinary given that America is and always has been a mongrel nation made up of various ethnicities, religions, and heritages. Despite the diversity, Chesterton surmised that Americans shared a similar mood reflecting a belief in the equality of all citizens. Chesterton could not decide whether this tenor was "the historic love of comrades or the last hysteria of the herd instinct," but he concluded that "there is the grandeur as well as the grave disadvantages of a natural catastrophe in that national unity." Few have been able to precisely define, however, exactly which values contribute to this unity. The values that Americans hold are as diverse as Americans themselves. Still, some of the principles rooted in Jeffersonian idealism continue to characterize the national outlook.

Because America was founded in rebellion, Americans have always emphasized freedom as a core aspect of national identity. Indeed, the American Revolution abolished the nation's attachment to monarchy and hierarchy and, in the words of author and scholar Seymour Martin Lipset, "enormously strengthened the individualistic, egalitarian, and anti-statist [sentiments] which had been present in the settler and religious background of the colonies." Since those times, freedom in America has remained a multifaceted value. It promotes individualism, the art of self-reliance that favors industry over idleness. It also entails egalitarianism, the notion that one can only enjoy liberty if it is shared by all. And finally, liberty in America suggests a distrust of state authority, a holdover from the abuses suffered under English rule. Libertarian thinkers connect this latter vision of liberty to the value of free markets. They assert that the colonists were especially troubled by the curtailment of market freedoms under the Crown, and therefore, Jefferson's concept of liberty included market freedoms as well as personal freedoms.

The free market ideals of competition and free enterprise are cherished values in America, especially in reinforcing the belief that Americans have the power to shape their own destiny through the application of hard work and ingenuity. The colonists, freed from the hereditary aristocracy of Europe, believed that all free men could be entrepreneurs and rise from poverty to comfort through the sweat of their own brow. Alexis de Tocqueville, the nineteenth-century French political thinker who witnessed the workings of American democracy during his tours of the United States, lauded this spirit of individualism and industriousness as defining elements of what he called American exceptionalism—those traits that differentiated the New World from the Old World. In enumerating several key values that persist in modern America, author Marc Pachter ties the notion of the self-made citizen to Americans' deep-seated love of choice. Pachter argues that although Americans are given privileges by birth or naturalization, most Americans "are assumed to be Americans by choice, not merely by historical legacy." Choosing to be an American implies choosing a life in which the individual can shape his or her own destiny. With this choosing, however, comes responsibility, in Pachter's view. "Americans may seem to be a nation of atomized individuals in social free-fall; but, in fact, they have not eliminated a sense of social obligation," Pachter claims. He sees Americans as exceptional because they are joiners and volunteers willing to help others who are not connected to them through family ties or through other affiliations.

Along with individualism and opportunity afforded by choice, Americans value privacy. L. Robert Kohls, who has written about the difficulties foreigners have in adjusting to American attitudes when visiting the United States, describes privacy as "the ultimate result of individualism" and a trait that can be difficult for foreigners to comprehend. Unlike many communal cultures in which privacy is often equated with loneliness and isolation, American culture values privacy "as a very positive condition," according to Kohls, one that is viewed "as a requirement which all humans would find equally necessary, desirable and satisfying." To Americans, privacy is linked to the notion of self-reliance and the resistance to authoritarianism. Interpreting the opinions of the Founders, many Americans prize privacy specifically as the right of the individual to be free of government intrusion, and in an era of increased government surveillance in response to the September 11, 2001, attacks on America, this view has gained wider currency among Americans of various political stripes.

As for Jefferson's other stipulated rights—life and the pursuit of happiness—scholars have filled these open-ended categories with a host of perceived American values. Many relate the pursuit of happiness to freedom of choice. That is, a person's happiness is an individual concern that is manifest in his or her choice of occupation, faith, and lifestyle. Others have shaded the pursuit of happiness to include emotional fulfillment. In the 1967 interracial marriage case *Loving v. Virginia*, the U.S. Supreme Court maintained that "the freedom to marry has long been recognized as one of the vital personal rights essential to the orderly pursuit of happiness by free men." Many Americans agree that marriage and family involvement are essential values that have given strength and order to the nation.

Conservative Christian organizations commonly promote marriage, family, and life as fundamental American values because these elements are important to their religious beliefs, and they assert that America's Founders accepted that the freedoms enjoyed in the New World were "endowed by their Creator." This has led many Christian conservatives to advocate faith as an American value. Faith-based values are important to Christian Americans, and this significance is evident during election times. In the election year of 2004, conservative Christian leader Jerry Falwell created the Faith and Values Coalition to support George W. Bush, the incumbent Republican president, and other government officeholders who advocated the values that the coalition cherished. Indeed, an exit poll revealed that more than 20 percent of voters in 2004 acknowledged that moral values were a deciding factor in choosing a candidate in the presidential race. Whether moral values should be equated with American values, however, is a point of contention in the nation. The enforced separation of church and state, along with the growth of other religions in America, has left many Americans skeptical of interpreting American values as divinely inspired.

In *Opposing Viewpoints: American Values*, social critics, politicians, and other commentators debate the values that are important to America and whether the country truly honors, protects, and lives by these principles. Chapters in this volume ask, "What Values Are Important to America?," "Are America's Values Threatened?," "How Should Patriotism Be Defined?," and "Can American Values Bridge Cultural Divides?" From these questions, one can comprehend some of the ideals that define America and have traditionally set it apart from other nations. Some of the viewpoints within these chapters, however, raise questions about whether American values have remained static or have adapted to changing times. As Marc Pachter notes, many countries have adopted democracy, rule of law, and free markets, and therefore their values may be quite similar to those held dear in the United States. Pachter writes, "Americans must begin to wonder how much the culture that once defined them as unique has become, in at least some of its aspects, the culture of global modernism." Perhaps de Tocqueville's concept of American exceptionalism defines an obsolete age, or perhaps, as many of the viewpoints in this anthology attest, the country must cling to its creed more tightly to ensure that its values are not sacrificed, subverted, or watered down in this global age.

OPPOSING
VIEWPOINTS®
SERIES

What Values Are Important to America?

Chapter Preface

In 1992, after a jury acquitted four Los Angeles police officers of misconduct for the beating of African American motorist Rodney King during a traffic stop, riots erupted across Los Angeles as predominantly black residents expressed anger at the verdict and long-standing antagonisms between the black community and the Los Angeles Police Department. Refusing to excuse the mayhem and violence as a justifiable reaction to the King case, Vice President Dan Quayle addressed the Commonwealth Club of California in the wake of the rioting to explain what he believed was the underlying motivation. Quayle said, "I believe the lawless social anarchy which we saw is directly related to the breakdown of family structure, personal responsibility and social order in too many areas of our society." He went on to quote statistics showing that black America was suffering from unprecedented numbers of fatherless families, illegitimate children, and incidents of homicide, but he suggested that the breakdown went beyond racial boundaries.

The vice president's solution to the decline of the family in America required citizens "to renew our public commitment to our Judeo-Christian values—in our churches and synagogues, our civic organizations and our schools." He insisted, "It's time to talk again about family, hard work, integrity and personal responsibility." Conservatives and the press picked up on Quayle's proposed remedy and started a national debate concerning the need to restore "family values" in the United States. The stalwart Christian segments of American society agreed with the vice president's summation, pushing the notion that a national commitment to traditional marriage, two-parent households, and premarital sexual abstinence would reaffirm America's moral strength. Many of these Americans believed that liberal elements in government had eroded the rightful place of religion as the nation's guiding force by enacting various laws that ranged from banning prayer in public schools to safeguarding gay rights. They used "family values" as a platform to promote the virtue of the nuclear family and a moral code based on Judeo-Christian ethics.

Critics of the Christianized concept of family values contend that the conservative project has less to do with building stronger families and more to do with disparaging atypical family structures such as single-parent households and same-sex marriages. Others, such as author and teacher Stephanie Coontz, challenge the fundamental belief that American families are declining from some idealized past. As Coontz writes, "No 'golden age' of the family can be found, and many of our ideals are based on a mythical family that never existed in the real world. The source of many of America's modern problems, moreover, both in and outside of the family, does not lie in a departure from old family practices and values but in the clash between unrealistic expectations and a changing socioeconomic environment." Coontz and other critics see the mission to reinvigorate family values as an attempt to scapegoat nontraditional families for social problems that have much deeper causes.

While many—including those in the pro-"family values" camp—maintain that the debate over family values is a global concern, Christian conservatives often link family values with American values. For example, the nonprofit organization American Values states that it champions the ideals of the Founding Fathers by aligning the nation's vision with "life, marriage, family, faith, and freedom." In the following chapter, commentators from various camps examine other ideals and philosophies that inform American values. Like family values, these concepts have been touted by one group or another as fundamental to American character and the ethical structure of the nation as a whole.

> *"Americans acknowledge that liberty is a gift of God, not an indulgence of government."*

Religious Freedom Strengthens America

Mitt Romney

Mitt Romney is a former Governor of Massachusetts (2002–2006) who unsuccessfully sought presidential candidacy in 2008 as a member of the Republican Party. In the following viewpoint, Romney explains how religion is both significant to America and to his potential bid for the office of president. Romney asserts that religion should not influence how politicians carry out their sworn duties to the nation, but he makes clear that this does not mean that government advocates a secular nation. The United States, Romney contends, was founded by men who believed that faith was a treasured value—one that was to be protected. He maintains that this conviction still guides the nation, assuring that most Americans are compassionate, tolerant defenders of liberty. For these reasons, Romney argues that the nation should not seek to eradicate God from the public sphere, nor should it back down from foreign aggressors who seek to impose a tyrannical version of faith upon the world.

Mitt Romney, "Faith in America," December 6, 2007. www.mittromney.com. Reproduced by permission.

As you read, consider the following questions:

1. According to Romney, what did young Abraham Lincoln describe as America's "political religion?"

2. According to Romney, in what way has the separation of church and state been taken well beyond its original meaning?

3. Of what does Romney think many European cathedrals have become a symbol?

"America faces a new generation of challenges. Radical violent Islam seeks to destroy us. An emerging China endeavors to surpass our economic leadership. And we are troubled at home by government overspending, overuse of foreign oil, and the breakdown of the family.

"Over the last year, we have embarked on a national debate on how best to preserve American leadership. Today, I wish to address a topic which I believe is fundamental to America's greatness: our religious liberty. I will also offer perspectives on how my own faith would inform my presidency, if I were elected.

"There are some who may feel that religion is not a matter to be seriously considered in the context of the weighty threats that face us. If so, they are at odds with the nation's founders, for they, when our nation faced its greatest peril, sought the blessings of the Creator. And further, they discovered the essential connection between the survival of a free land and the protection of religious freedom. In John Adams' words: 'We have no government armed with power capable of contending with human passions unbridled by morality and religion. . . . Our constitution was made for a moral and religious people.'

"Freedom requires religion just as religion requires freedom. Freedom opens the windows of the soul so that man can discover his most profound beliefs and commune with God. Freedom and religion endure together, or perish alone.

"Given our grand tradition of religious tolerance and liberty, some wonder whether there are any questions regarding an aspiring candidate's religion that are appropriate. I believe there are. And I will answer them today.

"Almost fifty years ago another candidate from Massachusetts explained that he was an American running for President, not a Catholic running for President. Like him, I am an American running for President. I do not define my candidacy by my religion. A person should not be elected because of his faith nor should he be rejected because of his faith.

"Let me assure you that no authorities of my church, or of any other church for that matter, will ever exert influence on presidential decisions. Their authority is them, within the province of church affairs, and it ends where the affairs of the nation begin.

"As governor, I tried to do the right as best I knew it, serving the law and answering to the Constitution. I did not confuse the particular teachings of my church with the obligations of the office and of the Constitution—and of course, I would not do so as president. I will put no doctrine of any church above the plain duties of the office and the sovereign authority of the law.

"As a young man, Lincoln described what he called America's 'political religion'—the commitment to defend the rule of law and the Constitution. When I place my hand on the Bible and take the oath of office, that oath becomes my highest promise to God. If I am fortunate to become your President, I will serve no one religion, no one group, no one cause, and no one interest. A president must serve only the common cause of the people of the United States.

"There are some for whom these commitments are not enough. They would prefer it if I would simply distance myself from my religion, say that it is more a tradition than my personal conviction, or disavow one or another of its precepts. That I will not do. I believe in my Mormon faith and I endeavor to live by it. My faith is the faith of my fathers—I will be true to them and to my beliefs.

"Some believe that such a confession of my faith will sink my candidacy. If they are right, so be it. But I think they underestimate the American people. Americans do not respect believers of convenience. Americans tire of those who would jettison their beliefs, even to gain the world.

"There is one fundamental question about which I often am asked. What do I believe about Jesus Christ? I believe that Jesus Christ is the Son of God and the Savior of mankind. My church's beliefs about Christ may not all be the same as those of other faiths. Each religion has its own unique doctrines and history. These are not bases for criticism but rather a test of our tolerance. Religious tolerance would be a shallow principle indeed if it were reserved only for faiths with which we agree.

"There are some who would have a presidential candidate describe and explain his church's distinctive doctrines. To do so would enable the very religious test the founders prohibited in the Constitution. No candidate should become the spokesman for his faith. For if he becomes president he will need the prayers of the people of all faiths.

"I believe that every faith I have encountered draws its adherents closer to God. And in every faith I have come to know, there are features I wish were in my own. I love the profound ceremony of the Catholic mass, the approachability of God in the prayers of the Evangelicals, the tenderness of spirit among the Pentecostals, the confident independence of the Lutherans, the ancient traditions of the Jews, unchanged through the ages, and the commitment to frequent prayer of the Muslims. As I travel across the country and see our towns and cities, I am always moved by the many houses of worship with their steeples, all pointing to heaven, reminding us of the source of life's blessings.

"It is important to recognize that while differences in theology exist between the churches in America, we share a common creed of moral convictions. And where the affairs of our nation are concerned, it's usually a sound role to focus on the latter—on the great moral principles that urge us all on a common course. Whether it was the cause of abolition, or civil rights, or the right to life itself, no movement of conscience can succeed in America that cannot speak to the convictions of religious people.

"We separate church and state affairs in this country, and for good reason. No religion should dictate to the state nor should the state interfere with the free practice of religion. But in recent years, the notion of the separation of church and state has been taken by some well beyond its original meaning. They seek to remove from the public domain any acknowledgment of God. Religion is seen as merely a private affair with no place in public life. It is as if they are intent on establishing a new religion in America—the religion of secularism. They are wrong.

"The founders proscribed the establishment of a state religion, but they did not countenance the elimination of religion from the public square. We are a nation 'Under God' and in God, we do indeed trust.

"We should acknowledge the Creator as did the Founders—in ceremony and word. He should remain on our currency, in our pledge, in the teaching of our history, and during the holiday season, nativity scenes and menorahs should be welcome in our public places. Our greatness would not long endure without judges who respect the foundation of faith upon which our Constitution rests. I will take care to separate the affairs of government from any religion, but I will not separate us from 'the God who gave us liberty.'

"Nor would I separate us from our religious heritage. Perhaps the most important question to ask a person of faith who seeks a political office, is this: does he share these Ameri-

The Relevancy of Religion Today

More than half of Americans think that traditional religions can answer all or most of today's problems. But a sizable minority sees traditional religions as less relevant to modern life: 32 percent say that traditional religions are old-fashioned and out of date.

TRADITIONAL RELIGIONS. . .

Can answer today's problems	54 percent
Are out of date	32 percent

White evangelical Christians are especially likely to see traditional religions as appropriate today—83 percent do. Nearly seven in ten Protestants see traditional religion as relevant to today's problems, as do 57 percent of Catholics. At the opposite end of the spectrum, seven in ten of those with no religion view traditional religion as old-fashioned.

CBS News Poll, April 13, 2006.

can values: the equality of human kind, the obligation to serve one another, and a steadfast commitment to liberty?

"They are not unique to any one denomination. They belong to the great moral inheritance we hold in common. They are the firm ground on which Americans of different faiths meet and stand as a nation, united.

"We believe that every single human being is a child of God—we are all part of the human family. The conviction of the inherent and inalienable worth of every life is still the most revolutionary political proposition ever advanced. John Adams put it that we are 'thrown into the world all equal and alike.'

"The consequence of our common humanity is our responsibility to one another, to our fellow Americans foremost, but also to every child of God. It is an obligation which is fulfilled by Americans every day, here and across the globe, without regard to creed or race or nationality.

"Americans acknowledge that liberty is a gift of God, not an indulgence of government. No people in the history of the world have sacrificed as much for liberty. The lives of hundreds of thousands of America's sons and daughters were laid down during the last century to preserve freedom, for us and for freedom loving people throughout the world. America took nothing from that century's terrible wars—no land from Germany or Japan or Korea; no treasure; no oath of fealty. America's resolve in the defense of liberty has been tested time and again. It has not been found wanting, nor must it ever be. America must never falter in holding high the banner of freedom.

"These American values, this great moral heritage, is shared and lived in my religion as it is in yours. I was taught in my home to honor God and love my neighbor. I saw my father march with Martin Luther King. I saw my parents provide compassionate care to others, in personal ways to people nearby, and in just as consequential ways in leading national volunteer movement. I am moved by the Lord's words: 'For I was an hungered, and ye gave me meat: I was thirsty, and ye gave me drink: I was a stranger, and ye took me in: naked, and ye clothed me . . .'

"My faith is grounded on these truths. You can witness them in Ann and my marriage and in our family. We are a long way from perfect and we have surely stumbled along the way, but our aspirations, our values, are the self-same as those from the other faiths that stand upon this common foundation. And these convictions will indeed inform my presidency.

"Today's generations of Americans have always known religious liberty. Perhaps we forget the long and arduous path our nation's forbearers took to achieve it. They came here from England to seek freedom of religion. But upon finding it for themselves, they at first denied it to others. Because of their diverse beliefs, Ann Hutchinson was exiled from Massachusetts Bay, a banished Roger Williams founded Rhode Island, and two centuries later, Brigham Young set out for the West. Americans were unable to accommodate their commitment to their own faith with an appreciation for the convictions of others to different faiths. In this, they were very much like those of the European nations they had left.

"It was in Philadelphia that our founding fathers defined a revolutionary vision of liberty, grounded on self-evident truths about the equality of all, and the inalienable rights with which each is endowed by his Creator.

"We cherish these sacred rights, and secure them in our Constitutional order. Foremost do we protect religious liberty, not as a matter of policy but as a matter of right. There will be no established church, and we are guaranteed the free exercise of our religion.

"I'm not sure that we fully appreciate the profound implications of our tradition of religious liberty. I have visited many of the magnificent cathedrals in Europe. They are so inspired . . . so grand . . . so empty. Raised up over generations, long ago, so many of the cathedrals now stand as the postcard backdrop to societies just too busy or too 'enlightened' to venture inside and kneel in prayer. The establishment of state religions in Europe did no favor to Europe's churches. And though you will find many people of strong faith there, the churches themselves seem to be withering away.

"Infinitely worse is the other extreme, the creed of conversion by conquest: violent Jihad, murder as martyrdom . . . killing Christians, Jews, and Muslims with equal indifference. These radical Islamists do their preaching not by reason or example, but in the coercion of minds and the shedding of blood. We face no greater danger today than theocratic tyranny, and the boundless suffering these states and groups could inflict if given the chance.

"The diversity of our cultural expression, and the vibrancy of our religious dialogue, has kept America in the forefront of civilized nations even as others regard religious freedom as something to be destroyed.

"In such a world, we can be deeply thankful that we live in a land where reason and religion are friends and allies in the cause of liberty, joined against the evils and dangers of the day. And you can be certain of this: Any believer in religious freedom, any person who has knelt in prayer to the Almighty, has a friend and ally in me. And so it is for hundreds of millions of our countrymen: we do not insist on a single strain of religion—rather, we welcome our nation's symphony of faith.

"Recall the early days of the First Continental Congress in Philadelphia, during the fall of 1774. With Boston occupied by British troops, there were rumors of imminent hostilities and fears of an impending war. In this time of peril, someone suggested that they pray. But there were objections. 'They were too divided in religious sentiments,' what with Episcopalians and Quakers, Anabaptists and Congregationalists, Presbyterians and Catholics.

"Then Sam Adams rose, and said he would hear a prayer from anyone of piety and good character, as long as they were a patriot.

"And so together they prayed, and together they fought, and together, by the grace of God . . . they founded this great nation.

"In that spirit, let us give thanks to the divine 'author of liberty.' And together, let us pray that this land may always be blessed, 'with freedom's holy light.'

'God bless the United States of America.'"

> "In a democracy, there should be no
> fixed truth except that everyone has the
> right to offer a new view—and to
> change his or her mind."

Religious Freedom Does Not Strengthen America

Ira Chernus

In the following viewpoint, Ira Chernus argues that politicians often use religion to assure voters of fundamental moral absolutes that can guide America through difficult times. In Chernus's view, this is a rhetorical ploy, but one that has a hidden agenda. By invoking the notion that America subscribes to shared religious values, politicians imply that citizens do not have the right or power to foster their own beliefs or question the supposed core values of the nation. Chernus sees this as a threat to democracy and an attempt to impose an "us versus them" mentality that would separate "true Americans" from those who may dissent. Ira Chernus is a professor of religious studies at the University of Colorado at Boulder.

As you read, consider the following questions:

1. In what way does Chernus see religious language in the political arena as "an end in itself?"

Ira Chernus, "Is Religion a Threat to Democracy? Faith Talk on the Campaign Trail," January 13, 2008. www.TomDispatch.com. Reproduced by permission of the author.

2. What does Chernus mean when he says, "All too often, the faith-talk view of freedom ends up taking away freedom?"

3. Why is it likely that words and symbols of moral absolutes have a conservative impact on a nation, according to the author?

It's a presidential campaign like no other. The [2008] candidates have been falling all over each other in their rush to declare the depth and sincerity of their religious faith. The pundits have been just as eager to raise questions that seem obvious and important: Should we let religious beliefs influence the making of law and public policy? If so, in what way and to what extent? Those questions, however, assume that candidates bring the subject of faith into the political arena largely to justify—or turn up the heat under—their policy positions. In fact, faith talk often has little to do with candidates' stands on the issues. There's something else going on here.

Look at the TV ad that brought [Republican candidate] Mike Huckabee out of obscurity in Iowa, the one that identified him as a "Christian Leader" who proclaims: "Faith doesn't just influence me. It really defines me." That ad did indeed mention a couple of actual political issues—the usual suspects, abortion and gay marriage—but only in passing. Then Huckabee followed up with a red sweater-themed Christmas ad that actively encouraged voters to ignore the issues. We're all tired of politics, the kindly pastor indicated. Let's just drop all the policy stuff and talk about Christmas—and Christ.

Ads like his aren't meant to argue policy. They aim to create an image—in this case, of a good Christian with a steady moral compass who sticks to his principles. At a deeper level, faith-talk ads work hard to turn the candidate—whatever candidate—into a bulwark of solidity, a symbol of certainty; their goal is to offer assurance that the basic rules for living remain fixed, objective truths, as true as religion.

People Look for Stability in Unstable Times

In a time when the world seems like a shaky place—whether you have a child in Iraq, a mortgage you may not be able to meet, a pension threatening to head south, a job evaporating under you, a loved one battling drug or alcohol addiction, an ex who just came out as gay or born-again, or a president you just can't trust—you may begin to wonder whether there is any moral order in the universe. Are the very foundations of society so shaky that they might not hold up for long? Words about faith—nearly any words—speak reassuringly to such fears, which haunt millions of Americans.

These fears and the religious responses to them have been a key to the political success of the religious right in recent decades. Randall Balmer, a leading scholar of evangelical Christianity, points out that it's offered not so much "issues" to mobilize around as "an unambiguous morality in an age of moral and ethical uncertainty."

[Republican candidate] Mitt Romney was courting the evangelical-swinging-toward-Huckabee vote when he, too, went out of his way to link religion with moral absolutes in his big Iowa speech on faith. Our "common creed of moral convictions. . . . the firm ground on which Americans of different faiths meet" turned out, utterly unsurprisingly, to be none other than religious soil: "We believe that every single human being is a child of God. . . . liberty is a gift of God." No doubts allowed here.

American politicians have regularly wielded religious language and symbolism in their moments of need, and such faith talk has always helped provide a sense of moral certainty in a shape-shifting world. But in the better years of the previous century, candidates used religion mostly as an adjunct to the real meat of the political process, a tool to whip up support for policies.

The Rhetoric of Certitude

How times have changed. Think of it, perhaps, as a way to measure the powerful sense of unsettledness that has taken a firm hold on American society. Candidates increasingly keep their talk about religion separate from specific campaign issues. They promote faith as something important and valuable in and of itself in the election process. They invariably avow the deep roots of their religious faith and link it not with issues, but with certitude itself.

Sometimes it seems that Democrats do this with even more grim regularity than Republicans. John Edwards, for example, reassured the nation that "the hand of God today is in every step of what happens with me and every human being that exists on this planet." In the same forum, Hillary Clinton proclaimed that she "had a grounding in faith that gave me the courage and the strength to do what I thought was right, regardless of what the world thought. And that's all one can expect or hope for."

When religious language enters the political arena in this way, as an end in itself, it always sends the same symbolic message: Yes, Virginia (or Iowa or New Hampshire or South Carolina) there *are* absolute values, universal truths that can never change. You are not adrift in a sea of moral chaos. Elect me and you're sure to have a fixed mooring to hold you and your community fast forever.

That message does its work in cultural depths that arguments about the separation of church and state can never touch. Even if the candidates themselves don't always understand what their words are doing, this is the biggest, most overlooked piece in today's faith and politics puzzle—and once you start looking for it, you find it nearly everywhere on the political landscape.

The Threat to Democracy

So, when it comes to religion and politics, here's the most critical question: Should we turn the political arena into a

The Influence of Religion in Politics

While most [Americans polled in a 2006 survey by the Pew Research Center] think religion's influence on American life is in decline, there is a division of opinion over whether religion's influence on government is rising or falling. About as many say religion is losing influence on government leaders and institutions, such as the president, Congress and Supreme Court (45 percent), as say religion's political influence is on the rise (42 percent).

Most of those who say that religion's influence on government is declining believe this is a bad thing. But Republicans and Democrats who perceive a growing religious influence on government differ over the impact of this trend. Overall, about a third of Republicans say religion's influence over government is growing, and by a wide margin (23 percent vs. 10 percent) they say this is a good thing for the country. Among Democrats, 45 percent say religion has a greater impact on government today, but they generally say this is a bad thing (28 percent) rather than a good thing (14 percent). Independents, for the most part, share the views of Democrats.

Pew Research Center for the People and the Press,
"Many Americans Uneasy with Mix of Religion and Politics,"
August 24, 2006.

stage to dramatize our quest for moral certainty? The simple answer is no—for lots of reasons.

For starters, it's a direct threat to democracy. The essence of our system is that we, the people, get to choose our values. We don't discover them inscribed in the cosmos. So everything must be open to question, to debate, and therefore to change. In a democracy, there should be no fixed truth except that everyone has the right to offer a new view—and to change his or her mind. It's a process whose outcome should never be predictable, a process without end. A claim to absolute truth—any absolute truth—stops that process.

For those of us who see the political arena as the place where the whole community gathers to work for a better world, it's even more important to insist that politics must be about large-scale change. The politics of moral absolutes send just the opposite message: Don't worry, whatever small changes are necessary, it's only in order to resist the fundamental crumbling that frightens so many. Nothing really important can ever change.

Many liberals and progressives hear that profoundly conservative message even when it's hidden beneath all the reasonable arguments about church and state. That's one big reason they are often so quick to sound a shrill alarm at every sign of faith-based politics.

They also know how easy it is to go from "there is a fixed truth" to "I have that fixed truth." And they've seen that the fixed truth in question is all too often about personal behaviors that ought to be matters of free choice in a democracy.

Which brings us to the next danger: Words alone are rarely enough to reassure the uncertain. In fact, the more people rely on faith talk to pursue certainty, the more they may actually reinforce both anxiety and uncertainty. It's a small step indeed to move beyond the issue of individual self-control to controlling others through the passage of laws.

Campaigns to put the government's hands on our bodies are not usually missionary efforts meant to make us accept someone else's religion. They are much more often campaigns to stage symbolic dramas about self-control and moral reassurance.

Controlling the Passions

American culture has always put a spotlight on the question: Can you control your impulses and desires—especially sexual desires—enough to live up to the moral rules? As a historian of religion, John F. Wilson tells us, the quest for surety has typically focused on a "control of self" that "through discipline" finally becomes self-control. In the 2008 presidential campaign, this still remains true. Listen, for example, to [Democratic candidate] Barack Obama: "My Bible tells me that if we train a child in the way he should go, when he is old he will not turn from it. So I think faith and guidance can help fortify . . . a sense of reverence that all young people should have for the act of sexual intimacy."

Mitt Romney fit snugly into the same mold. He started his widely-heralded statement on religion by talking about a time when "our nation faced its greatest peril," a threat to "the survival of a free land." Was he talking about terrorism? No. He immediately went on to warn that the real danger comes from "human passions unbridled." Only morality and religion can do the necessary bridling, he argued, quoting John Adams to make his case: "Our constitution was made for a moral and religious people"—in other words, people who can control themselves. That's why "freedom requires religion."

All too often, though, the faith-talk view of freedom ends up taking away freedom. When Romney said he'd be "delighted" to sign "a federal ban on all abortions," only a minority of Americans approved of that position (if we can believe the polls), but it was a sizable minority. For them, fear of unbridled passion is stronger than any commitment to personal freedom.

In the end, it may be mostly their own passions that they fear. But since the effort to control oneself is frustrating, it can easily turn into a quest for "control over other selves," to quote historian Wilson again, "with essentially bipolar frameworks for conceiving of the world: good versus bad, us versus them"—"them" being liberals, secular humanists, wild kids, or whatever label the moment calls for.

The upholders of virtue want to convince each other that their values are absolutely true. So they stick together and stand firm against those who walk in error. As Romney put it, "Any person who has knelt in prayer to the Almighty has a friend and ally in me."

That's the main dynamic driving the movements to ban abortion and gay marriage. But they're just the latest in a long line of such movements, including those aimed at prohibiting or restricting alcohol, drugs, gambling, birth control, crime, and other behaviors that are, in a given period, styled as immoral.

Us versus Them

Since it's always about getting "them" to control their passions, the target is usually personal behavior. But it doesn't have to be. Just about any law or policy can become a symbol of eternal moral truth—even foreign policy, one area where liberals, embarked on their own faith-talk campaigns, are more likely to join conservatives.

The bipartisan war on terror has, for instance, been a symbolic drama of "us versus them," acting out a tale of moral truth. [Former Mayor of New York City] Rudolph Giuliani made the connection clear shortly after the 9/11 attack when he went to the United Nations to whip up support for that "war." "The era of moral relativism . . . must end," he demanded. "Moral relativism does not have a place in this discussion and debate."

Nor does it have a place in the current campaign debate about foreign policy. Candidate Huckabee, for example, has no hesitation about linking war abroad to the state of morality here at home. He wants to continue fighting in Iraq, he says, because "our way of life, our economic and moral strength, our civilization is at stake. . . . I am determined to look this evil in the eye, confront it, defeat it." As his anti-gay marriage statement asks, "What's the point of keeping the terrorists at bay in the Middle East, if we can't keep decline and decadence at bay here at home?"

On the liberal side, the theme is more muted but still there. Barack Obama, for instance, has affirmed that the U.S. *must* "lead the world in battling immediate evils and promoting the ultimate good. I still believe that America is the last, best hope of Earth." Apparently that's why we need to keep tens of thousands of troops in Iraq indefinitely. Clinton calls for "a bipartisan consensus to ensure our interests, increase our security and advance our values," acting out "our deeply-held desire to remake the world as it ought to be." Apparently that's why, in her words, "we cannot take any option off the table in sending a clear message to the current leadership of Iran."

When words and policies become symbols of moral absolutes, they are usually about preventing some "evil" deed or turning things back to the way they (supposedly) used to be. So they are likely to have a conservative impact, even when they come from liberals.

Freedom Without Faith Talk

In itself, faith in politics poses no great danger to democracy as long as the debates are really about policies—and religious values are translated into political values, articulated in ways that can be rationally debated by people who don't share them. The challenge is not to get religion out of politics. It's to get the quest for certitude out of politics.

The first step is to ask why that quest seems increasingly central to our politics today. It's not simply because a right-wing cabal wants to impose its religion on us. The cabal exists, but it's not powerful enough to shape the political scene on its own. That power lies with millions of voters across the political spectrum. Candidates talk about faith because they want to win votes.

Voters reward faith talk because they want candidates to offer them symbols of immutable moral order. The root of the problem lies in the underlying insecurities of voters, in a sense of powerlessness that makes change seem so frightening, and control—especially of others—so necessary.

The only way to alter that condition is to transform our society so that voters will feel empowered enough to take the risks, and tolerate the freedom that democracy requires. That would be genuine change. It's a political problem with a political solution. Until that solution begins to emerge, there is no way to take the conservative symbolic message of faith talk out of American politics.

> "Acting in accordance with our Christian beliefs, the free market system allows for creation of wealth by enhancing and improving what God has given us through strong work ethics."

Capitalism Promotes Freedom and Opportunity

Bob Ditmar

In the following viewpoint, Bob Ditmar contends that capitalism is "the most moral economic system derived by man." According to Ditmar, America's free market economy allows citizens to reap the rewards of hard work—obtaining necessities while building wealth. He also asserts that capitalism benefits the nation by promoting technological innovation, medical advances, and job creation. In Ditmar's view, capitalism is even in accord with Christian values by helping to bring about economic justice and fostering a sense of social responsibility to the less fortunate. Robert Ditmar is the author of an editorial column in the American Daily, *a conservative Internet periodical.*

Bob Ditmar, "Euro-Skeptics and Arab Discontent: In Defense of the American System," *American Daily*, April 20, 2003. Reproduced by permission of the author.

As you read, consider the following questions:

1. In Ditmar's opinion, what is the "Old Europe" perspective of America's success and its relationship to capitalism?

2. What three nations does Ditmar say would be "backward, impoverished agrarian societies" if it were not for their embrace of free market economies?

3. In what way does capitalism not attempt to "play God," as Ditmar explains?

The hatred and abuse that the United States is experiencing from continental Europe and the Arab-Muslim world is mostly out of envy and an excuse for the failure of their own systems.

The world has seen the failure of fascism, socialism, communism, Islamism and many other "isms" during the past 100 years. With the fall of global communism, especially in the old Soviet bloc, the main system still standing virtually unchallenged is the American free market capitalist system. This system, which first took root in the New World prior to the foundation of the United States as a nation-state, not only continues to exist, but is thriving after nearly 400 years.

While the American free-market system is often criticized by various quarters of the world, particularly the liberals, Islamic leaders and anarchists of western continental Europe and secular Arab and Islamic dictatorship-theocracies, there are really no serious contending systems that can truly challenge it. And the more these totalitarian and socialist systems actually realize this, the more they begin to hold the United States in total contempt, trumping up charges of "unilateralism" in the face of "international consensus." However, the real foundation of this hatred by the likes of France, Germany, Iran, Syria, and the "Arab street" is not so much the American determination to live and act as a sovereign nation acting in its own best interest, as it is envy of America's total dominating success in all arenas it chooses to participate.

European and Arab Views of American Capitalism

In Old Europe's perspective, America does not have the enlightened sophistication, and therefore has not the right to the power and influence it has amassed in an incredibly short span of time. After all, European culture is 2,000 years old while America has existed as a nation-state for only 227 years [as of 2003]. In many European eyes, America's success has not occurred because of any particular U.S. constitutional free-market based system so much as it was merely a continuance of European ideals and innovation simply transplanted across the Atlantic. To France and Germany, America owes all of its power, wealth and influence to the slow process of a growing civilization that is Europe. In essence, these Europeans view the success of America as more of an artificial success, built upon what they view as an artificial culture and stolen from the solid cultural and intellectual European foundation. It is this European foundation then, upon which American success is truly built. Therefore, in the viewpoint of Old Europe, the United States has absolutely no right to act in any way, for any reason, even in its own interests, unless it first consults with, and gets permission from, the international community (read: France, Germany, and the United Nations).

In the case of the Arab-Muslim nations in the Middle East and Africa, this argument is taken back even further. In the eyes of these nations, European and Western dominance, in the form of colonial empires, stole the wealth and resources of the ancient cultures and intellectual capital that took thousands of years to acquire. Thus, what today is called the "Third World" was essentially put into a permanent disadvantaged state as a result of colonial imperialism. They can never expect to come up to the standards of the developed nations and have lowered their own expectations of ever getting to "First World" status. The colonial excuse is an easy scapegoat to avoid making the tough decisions a government must make to position its resources and pull itself out of poverty.

Many of today's dictatorships and Islamist radicals, including the recently ousted tyrant, Saddam Hussein, of Iraq, use slogans denouncing Western and American "imperialism" as a way to sell their totalitarian ideologies to their people and keep them under tight control. Influence from the West is nothing more than a continuance of colonialism through modern means. In Arab-Muslim eyes, America is nothing but an extension of the old European colonial powers using stolen resources to dominate the Arab world militarily, economically and culturally. Using the excuse of American imperialism and exploitation of the region's oil resources as an excuse for their poverty and failures, these Middle Eastern dictatorships continue to oppress their people. Under the pretense of protecting their populations from morally decadent American culture, Muslim theocracies allow no freedom of expression or creativity. The result is a lack of entrepreneurial motivation or innovation that can create a better economic condition for these oppressed nations. Instead, it creates a continuing cycle of hatred, envy, poverty and violence. These failures are conveniently misplaced on the United States and the West.

America Is Still the Model of Success

Today we see the spread of the American capitalist and free market system to many of these former Communist nations, such as Russia and Eastern Europe. Even in countries today that still claim to be Communist in theory, such as China and Vietnam, people are openly engaging in capitalism. But the increasing gap between the older, wealthier Western and capitalist nations to those of the Second and Third World still make capitalism the appealing target of choice for criticism from the intellectuals and elitists of the political Left. They argue that capitalism is a system of moral decay, fraud, theft and outright oppression. They base their argument that our abundance has created such resentment in the Arab-Islamic world that the frustrations have simply "boiled over" to the point of our deserving what they term the "tragic events" of September 11, 2001. However, I will argue that the American free trade system, also known as "capitalism," is the most moral economic system derived by man. It's not perfect, but no other system has come close.

Accusing American capitalism and colonialism as the root of all the world's poverty, ills and evils is a convenient weapon in the arsenal of the "Blame America for Everything" crowd. However, if this is aberrantly the case, then how is it possible that many former colonial nations, such as South Korea, Singapore, Canada, Australia, and even the United States have all become prosperous despite their colonial pasts? Why don't we see former Soviet bloc nations that have recently shaken the chains of tyranny emulating European socialistic systems or Muslim theocracies? Why do nations emerging from the darkness of totalitarianism most often try to model their new economic and governmental systems after the American system? The answer lies in the success of the American system, based not on imperialism or exploitation, but rather its principled approach based on Judeo-Christian values.

Free Markets Provide Opportunity and Advancement

Capitalism allows for creation of wealth, basic necessities, goods and services, motivation, elimination of hunger, improvements, etc. The lack of central planning and control, letting supply and demand dictate what will be sold at what price, and the concept of a laissez-faire approach to commerce makes the environment ripe for advancements in food production, distribution of goods, technological advances, medical breakthroughs, creation of jobs and employment and higher wages.

As a result of a free market economy, people have motivation to take risks, hoping to reap the benefits of their risk, hard work, and innovation. Were it not for this system, Japan, South Korea and even China would today be backward, impoverished agrarian societies. For in capitalism, those entrepreneurs that were willing to work and take the risks thrived and created jobs and opportunities for those who could not take risks and otherwise would not have income. In time, some of those benefactors of employment created by the risk-takers would get ideas to improve on something and in turn would take the risks of starting their own businesses. Because more people had jobs and, therefore, the income it generated afforded many more to get an education that otherwise may not have. This cycle continues through the decades to the present day.

This "chain reaction" of entrepreneural spirit sometimes includes failed ventures, but because the motivation, freedom to be innovative, and the rewards of the promise of success were there, these societies were able to pull themselves up from the dust of World War II and the Korean War into the top tier of the Industrialized World today. The governments are democratic and allow for this innovation to continue, as elsewhere in the Industrial First World. As a result, in the First World real poverty is nonexistent, literacy and education are almost 100 percent attainable, and advancements and innovations in technology, food production, medicine, and standards of living continue to explode. All people in these systems benefit and all are able to partake of God's bounty because of this freedom.

Improving on God's Bounty

From an ethical standpoint, I believe the free market system is the most logical system based upon the belief that there are universal moral truths and principles. In many ways, capitalism is based upon many of our Christian values of creation,

Economic Power Is a Check to Political Power

The characteristic feature of action through political channels is that it tends to require or enforce substantial conformity. The great advantage of the market, on the other hand, is that it permits wide diversity. It is, in political terms, a system of proportional representation. Each man can vote, as it were, for the color of tie he wants and get it; he does not have to see what color the majority wants and then, if he is in the minority, submit.

It is this feature of the market that we refer to when we say that the market provides economic freedom. But this characteristic also has implications that go far beyond the narrowly economic. Political freedom means the absence of coercion of a man by his fellow men. The fundamental threat to freedom is power to coerce, be it in the hands of a monarch, a dictator, an oligarchy, or a momentary majority. The preservation of freedom requires the elimination of such concentration of power to the fullest possible extent and the dispersal and distribution of whatever power cannot be eliminated—a system of checks and balances. By removing the organization of economic activity from the control of political authority, the market eliminates this source of coercive power. It enables economic strength to be a check to political power rather than a reinforcement.

Milton Friedman,
Capitalism and Freedom, *1962.*

the Golden Rule, and many of God's commandments. Acting in accordance with our Christian beliefs, the free market system allows for creation of wealth by enhancing and improving what God has given us through strong work ethics. Capitalism as a system gives more food, medical and monetary aid to poor nations than do other economic systems. This is in accordance with the principle of those that are blessed by God with wealth should not keep all for themselves, but strive to help those that are poor by always trying to give aid and help to bring those that are poor up to the standards of the wealthier. It is attempting to bring about economic justice to all. Everyone has a "right" as endowed by our Creator, to life, liberty, freedom of thought and deed, and the pursuit of happiness. Only capitalism recognizes that these principles are endowed by God and strives to give all mankind the access to live up to these God-given principles. Capitalism does not attempt to "play God," by telling people what to think, do, or act on, but instead attempts to give all a sense of awareness, social responsibility and develop individual's conscience to strive for doing good. Capitalism wants everyone to succeed by virtue of God-given talents and hard work. Ethically, this means capitalism, more than any other, attempts to follow the Golden Rule of "doing unto others as you would want to have done to you."

By contrast, in much of the Third World and the Arab World, societies lag far behind the First World not because of the evils of capitalism, but because of the total lack of freedom in the Islamic Sharia laws, akin to fascism, and the planned economies and atheism of many socialist countries such as North Korea. The contrast between the Koreas cannot be clearer. Both countries are geographically wed on a small peninsula, sharing the same few resources. However, the South's people thrive under capitalism while the North, under a planned central economy, allows millions of its people to starve to death while allocating the nation's resources for military purposes. The distribution system means that all the food aid and resources from the West cannot get to the people in these counties.

Good Governance Aids Capitalism

Corrupt governments, such as North Korea, the Palestinian Authority, the dictatorship of Iraq, and even the House of Saud, are the real reasons that these planned systems do not work. These governments misallocate their resources for selfish interests at the expense of their people. They encourage, using the facade of faith, that it is Western capitalism that causes their misery and therefore spreads the viral that creates "atrocities" such as September 11. Until the corrupt governments give way to open democratic societies, no economic system can ever be successful.

The types of socialist or corrupt theological and secular dictatorships I mention seemingly attempt to conflict with God's intended principles. In many cases, atheist socialism tells man that everything is simply "random" and that God is nothing but a way to keep mankind down. Islamic theocracy, under the cover of "serving Allah," actually uses dictatorial methods to instead take the place of God by taking away individuals' endowed rights as given by our Creator and instilling authoritarian methods of governing people. These systems lie, treat people in direct violation of the Golden Rule, and do everything possible to keep a lock on power over the masses. There is no pursuit of happiness, only a constant promise of "utopia" through endless five-year plans and eternal jihad against the infidels. And despite capitalism's continual aid to these poor nations under these systems, instead of allowing for the freedoms to persist to make these places thrive, the leaders in positions of power simply blame the capitalist societies for their own place in the hierarchy of the world economic system. They have no shame as long as they can keep tight control of their own people by blaming foreign governments, especially the West, for all the problems of their nations. To them, nothing is ever self-inflicted.

Free democratic capitalism brings about a way for all to come to a higher living standard. It is not about "leaving people behind to benefit the rich." It does not cause the gap between rich and poor nations. It is about creation. It is about the freedom [of] every person to find opportunities, develop and create other opportunities, and to develop their full human potential as endowed by God.

| "America embodies ruthless exploitation
of humanity and the Earth."

Capitalism Promotes Enslavement and Exploitation

Jason Miller

Jason Miller is the associate editor of Cyrano's Journal, *a media watchdog Internet periodical that exposes capitalist control of government in hopes of returning democracy to the people. Miller argues in the following viewpoint that capitalism has turned America into a plutocracy, a government run by the wealthy. He contends that while consumerism is meant to pacify the majority of Americans, it has made few wealthy and left many poor. The injustice of the capitalist system, in Miller's view, has crippled those on the lowest rung of the economic ladder, leaving millions homeless and depriving many more of basic necessities. And because "rags to riches" opportunities are but pipe dreams to Miller, he maintains that the majority of the impoverished can never escape their plight once they have reached that lowest rung.*

As you read, consider the following questions:

1. According to Miller, how have Horatio Alger stories supported the myths propagated by capitalism in America?

Jason Miller, "American Capitalism and the Moral Poverty of Nations: Of Faustian Bargains and Disposable Human Beings," *Thomas Paine's Corner*, May 29, 2006. Reproduced by permission.

2. As Miller reports, what value in assets are held by the
   wealthiest Americans?

3. What four economic factors does Miller say are "leaving
   many Americans vulnerable to financial disaster?"

Rolling through virtually any reasonably populous city or
town in America, one encounters a surreal landscape
blighted by grotesque temples to America's twin gods of capitalism and consumerism. As an increasing number of individual proprietors are driven to extinction, Wal-Mart,
McDonald's, and hundreds more leviathan corporations continue their rapid construction of more houses of worship to
serve their zealous congregation. Once inside, many Americans gleefully sacrifice an abundance of their greenbacks at al-
tars attended by consumerism's unwitting acolytes.

For appallingly meager wages and benefits, the cashiers
tending the sacred churches of capitalism and consumerism
gather the offerings which enable their fellow faithful to reap
the fruits of practicing their devotion.

Good little consumers can receive a veritable cornucopia
of "blessings" which include working in jobs amounting to in-
dentured servitude, obesity, insurmountable debt, insularity
from the rest of the world, unwitting support of a merciless
militaristic regime which is evolving into fascism, idolatrous
worship of celebrities and money, facilitation of obscene concentration of wealth into the hands of a few, and participation
in the severe desecration of our environment.

They may exist in a spiritual wasteland, but at least those
Americans who are fortunate enough to find themselves in
the shrinking middle class have access to basic human necessities, some creature comforts, and relative stability and safety
(at least for the short term). However, a growing number of
Americans find themselves wandering in a barren desert, lacking both sustenance for the soul and the corporeal "blessings"
bestowed upon the middle class wage earners by the high
priests of capitalism and consumerism. . . .

America Is a Plutocracy

Founded on the principles of individual liberty and self-determination (for White male property owners), the nascent United States provided fertile ground for the seeds of Capitalism. Conditions such as slavery, explosive growth in the number of banks, America's powerful drive to expand its territory, neutral trade during the war between Great Britain and France, and ultimately, the Industrial Revolution enabled American capitalism to grow into a thriving jungle.

By the late nineteenth century, trusts and monopolies flourished. Laissez-faire economic policy prevented the government "of the people" from meddling in the wealthy elite's obscene human and environmental exploitation. America's plutocracy was living large while the rest of the population struggled and suffered.

For years, America's schools and media have inculcated us with the notion that capitalism is the superlative socioeconomic system in the history of humankind. In spite of the "feel good" propaganda intended to keep us pacified, working, and consuming, there is a very dark side to the much vaunted American Way.

> America's abundance was created not by public sacrifices to the common good, but by the productive genius of free men who pursued their own personal interests and the making of their own private fortunes.

Thank you, Ayn Rand [author and advocate of capitalism], for affirming the naked brutality and avarice of America's socioeconomic system, a system which enables a privileged few who "play the game" well to mercilessly pursue their personal interests, amass private fortunes, and hoard the lion's share of "America's abundance."

People Are Commodities

The economy of the United States, which possesses many elements of commonly accepted definitions of capitalism, is tempered to some degree by components which would more appropriately be attributed to socialism or Progressive Utilization Theory (PROUT), socioeconomic systems devoted in large part to ensuring the welfare of society as a whole and which value humans as sentient beings rather than commodities.

Unfortunately, by and large, capitalism predominates in the American socioeconomic system and represents a substantial portion of our national character (or lack thereof). America embodies ruthless exploitation of humanity and the Earth. In the capitalist paradigm, human beings and the planet are simply material objects which exist to fulfill the desires of the bourgeoisie masters. Imperialism and neoliberalism go hand in glove with capitalism. Insatiable greed and objectification do not respect borders or boundaries. . . .

Only a Few Strike It Rich

Horatio Alger wrote over 130 very popular fiction novels in the nineteenth century. Unfortunately, his ideal notions of attaining "rags to riches" success through hard work and determination in the capitalist system were principally fiction too. Calling him a useful idiot would be unfair because his heart was in the right place, but his works did provide very useful propaganda for the wealthy ruling class who wanted their modern day serfs to believe they had a realistic chance of rising to the top of the economic or political food chain. Undeniably there are those who started with virtually nothing and accrued vast fortunes or became powerful people, but for each one who did, millions failed. And the same is true today.

Consider that over half of our presidents came from families ranking amongst the wealthiest 3 percent of Americans while at least a dozen sprang from the loins of elitists in the top 1 percent.

In 2005, 143 of 435 U.S. representatives and one in three senators were millionaires.

Statistics from 2002 indicate that eight of the fifteen wealthiest individuals in America had acquired their fortunes through inheritance. Five of these eight were Waltons [owners of the Wal-Mart chain]. The other three were progeny of the founder of the Mars Candy empire. Three of the top fifteen derived their fortunes from the same company, Microsoft. No concentration of wealth in the hands of a few there, is there?

Reports from 2002 also indicate that Bill Gates [co-founder of Microsoft] had acquired as much wealth as the bottom 40 percent of U.S. households. And the Walton clan possessed 771,287 times the wealth of the average U.S. household. Here is to the land of equal opportunity!

In 2004, the United States had 374 billionaires and 7.5 million millionaires (about 2 percent of the population). The wealthiest Americans possessed $11 trillion in assets. Meanwhile 13 percent of Americans lived below poverty level. What was that Horatio Alger myth again?

Yes, the bourgeoisie is thriving and dominating in the United States. We are indeed experiencing the dawn of the Second Gilded Age.

Who Reaps the Bounty

According to Friedrich Engels, the bourgeoisie are:

> . . . the class of modern capitalists, owners of the means of social production and employers of wage labour.

Whose function is:

> . . . the appropriation and therefore control of the labour of others and . . . the selling of the products of this labour.

And who are differentiated from the small proprietors (which their massive corporate entities often crush) by:

> capitalist production requires an individual capital big enough to employ a fairly large number of workers at a

Capitalists Are Recipients of the New Welfare

Corporate America, ironically, has become the heart of our welfare state, its huge subsidies from taxpayers far overshadowing the relatively small amounts provided to poor women and children. President [Ronald] Reagan's "welfare queen" with a Cadillac has been replaced by the corporate CEO with his exorbitant salary and perks. In short, the capitalist system is running wild, unfettered by reasonable rules and regulations, not constrained and balanced by the other forces of our society.

What is surprising is not that this development has occurred, but that it has occurred without much concern on the part of nonprofit organizations. The major reason for this inattention, of course, is that foundations and wealthy donors have continually refused to provide support for any systematic effort to monitor, assess, hold accountable, and improve the behavior of corporate America.

Pablo Eisenberg,
Chronicle of Philanthropy,
April 7, 2006.

time; only when he himself is wholly released from labour does the employer of labour become a full-blooded capitalist.

More staggering statistics demonstrate who reaps the bounty in a capitalist system (even one constrained by elements of more just and humane economic systems):

More than 99 percent of American businesses have fewer than 500 employees and account for less than 37 percent of all business sales.

Elite corporations (those employing more than 5,000 people) comprise a fraction of the remaining 1 percent of American businesses, yet ring up over 40 percent of sales.

Within specific business sectors, corporate monopolists shine brightly. The fifty largest banks control over 35 percent of bank assets in the United States.

The largest 100 corporations alone account for over 46 percent of corporate net income after taxes.

1 percent of Americans own more stock than the 90 percent of us who dwell at the bottom of Bush's "ownership society."

While a tiny segment of the U.S. population becomes increasingly powerful both economically and politically, working class families continue to rely on two incomes to make ends meet while 13 percent of the population lives below the poverty level.

As the semblance of a meritocracy in America succumbs to the forces of plutocratic ambition and greed under the [George W.] Bush Regime, American economic system's "noble and fair" reputation is dutifully maintained by genuflecting mainstream media pundits. Yet there is one particularly shameful stain which not even master propagandists can mask.

The Failed Promise of the American Dream

In a self-proclaimed Christian nation awash in a sea of money, guided by allegedly noble principles, and purported to have a Manifest Destiny to convert the world to the American Way, a significant number of discarded, hopelessly poor human beings are living proof of the cruel hypocrisy of the ruling elite of the United States. America's homeless are living testaments to the gross injustices of capitalism, even in an economy tempered with elements of government-funded social programs and regulations on businesses. . . .

Each year 3.5 million Americans experience homelessness. Of these unfortunates, 750,000 are chronically homeless. Forty-nine percent are Black while only 35 percent are White (which represents an obviously gross disproportion when compared to the racial make-up of the general population). A startling 40 percent of the homeless include families.

Homelessness is not limited to the conventional notion of people sleeping in a cardboard box or on a park bench. America's homeless people include those who live in their cars, abandoned buildings, cheap motels called flophouses, and train or bus stations.

Many homeless maintain jobs making sub-standard wages. Other ways the homeless obtain their meager incomes are through begging, street performance, selling street magazines (written and distributed by the homeless), and selling their blood plasma. In their desperation, some feign illness to gain admission to hospitals while others commit crimes so they can get "three hots and a cot. . . ."

Representing a particularly searing indictment of America's capitalist constitutional republic are the 500,000 U.S. military veterans who experience homelessness each year. Conscripted or manipulated by propaganda to fight in wars of imperial aggression (like Vietnam), homeless veterans were used by the elites and cast aside like yesterday's garbage. The Veterans Administration only provides housing for veterans who are chronically ill, has severely neglected the needs of those with mental illness, and cut most Vietnam War veterans adrift with no job training. Risk your life to expand the American Empire and you get to spend the rest of your days eating out of trash dumpsters.

Many choose homelessness, at least temporarily, because they are unable to make a living wage in America's "booming" economy or find themselves completely unemployed. Offshoring of American jobs, stagnant wages, the soaring cost of housing, and the agonizing loss of industrial sector jobs with healthy wages are leaving many Americans vulnerable to financial disaster. Overwhelmed by bills and crippled by insufficient income, some Americans are forced to choose amongst basic necessities. Naturally housing goes before food and clothing, leaving people living on the street, or if they are lucky, in their cars. . . .

Criminalizing Capitalism's Victims

As the moneyed class strengthens its dominance over our society, the plight of the homeless is worsening. The U.S. Conference of Mayors (representing 270 cities) reported that the demand for homeless shelter space increased by 13 percent in 2001 and by 25 percent in 2005. Twenty-two percent of those seeking shelter in 2005 were refused.

Demonstrating the depths of their compassion, our "benevolent" leaders have begun to criminalize homelessness. Of the 224 American cities that participated in a recent National Coalition for the Homeless survey, approximately 30 percent are taking measures targeting the homeless, including banning pan-handling and "camping," initiating frequent police sweeps of public areas to arrest or "evict" homeless persons, and selectively enforcing loitering laws.

While our heavily entrenched corporate elites and affluent decision-makers cut their own taxes, reduce spending on social programs, and lavish insane amounts of the working poor's and middle class's tax money on a military which exists to protect and expand their pecuniary interests, they offer the weakest members of our society, our homeless people, a quality of life that would repulse a sewer rat.

Thanks to the pathological greed unleashed and rewarded by Capitalism, America has forged a Faustian Pact [selling one's soul to the devil]. It is inevitable that Mephistopheles will come to collect his due. Or perhaps he already has.

▌ *"Let's put our faith back in people."*

American Democracy Should Be Renewed

Andrei Cherny

Democracy in America should mean putting authority back in the hands of the people, Andrei Cherny states in the following viewpoint. Cherny claims that American democracy has become a slave to corporate interests for a century and has cemented the connection between power and wealth. He advocates that the people regain control of the reins of government and steer the nation back toward the Jeffersonian ideal that democracy should ensure the greatest happiness for the masses and not just for an elite few. Andrei Cherny is co-founder and co-editor of Democracy: A Journal of Ideas, *a quarterly periodical of progressive politics.*

As you read, consider the following questions:

1. What were some of the parts of Jefferson's notion of radical democracy, as Cherny explains them?

2. What percentage of all Americans hold a third of the nation's worth, according to the author?

3. For what reasons does Cherny think modern times are well suited to reinvigorating democracy in America?

Andrei Cherny, "A New American Democracy," *Huffington Post*, January 11, 2006. Reproduced by permission of the author.

In America we've always had a deeper definition of democracy than just showing up at the ballot box once every couple of years.

America is a nation built upon a notion: that we're all created equal and all endowed with equal rights. That we each have an inalienable right to choose our own course, blaze our own path, rise as far as our talents can take us, walk shoulder to shoulder with anyone and be able to look them square in the eye. That's what we mean when we talk about democracy.

This was the faith of our founders. It is a faith they never wholly lived up to, a faith that we have always struggled to live by, and a faith that is today under attack.

Jefferson's Ideal

That faith was forged in the America of the agricultural age. When Thomas Jefferson was elected in 1800, America was a nation of farms and small towns. On the cold March morning he was inaugurated as president, he awoke at Mrs. Conrad's boarding house in Washington, D.C. He got dressed, went downstairs for breakfast and took his usual seat at the long table where all the boarders ate—the seat farthest from the warm fire. Someone got up and offered him a better seat. He smiled and refused.

Then he walked up the hill to the half-finished Capitol building and made his way up the steps. If he paused at the top, this would have been his view: seven or eight boarding houses, a tailor's, a shoemaker's, a printer's, an oyster market, a grocery shop, a stationery store, a dry goods store, a washwoman's home. And that was it. Nothing else. Just an endless expanse of dense forests and fertile fields. America was an undiscovered country, an untrammeled wilderness where every step forward was an exploration, where a young man could set out in a New World with the confidence that no one was coming up behind him and no one stood in his way.

So Jefferson put forward a radically democratic vision that fit the times. He said, the purpose of government was "to secure the greatest degree of happiness possible to the general mass of those associated under it." And to do that we needed to expand the right to vote to the poor as well as the rich. That we had to give everyone land so they could farm and build their own opportunity and create strong communities. He bought the Louisiana Territory so that more people could get a piece of that opportunity. And he sent Lewis and Clark west on a voyage of discovery.

Throughout the century, Jefferson's heirs continued to create a democracy defined by equality and opportunity—with the Oregon Trail and the Homestead Act and the land grant colleges. . . .

End of Agrarianism

But that America began to slip away. Where the word "boss" didn't exist in Jefferson's day, by the 1860s 40 percent of America worked for someone else. And by 1920, 87 percent of wage earners not only worked for a boss but for a new thing called a corporation.

Why? Because the world had changed and the rules of American life had changed with it.

A century ago, people were moving from farms to factories, from the country to the city, from independence to interdependence. . . .

[In the nineteenth century] Jefferson's heirs—the people who believed in progress and equality and opportunity for all—the defenders of American democracy—watched as a new economy and the people twisting it for their own purposes undermined all their achievements of the previous century. As all their progress and work was threatened.

And they had a choice. They could rail against change and defend to the death what had come before. Or they could build on the past and achieve their goals in new ways in a new century.

And those who believed in democracy were split. Some chose the first path: they attacked as criminals all those who were undermining the Jefferson's ways of thinking. They sought to preserve yesterday's America at any cost. In his famous Cross of Gold speech accepting the Democratic nomination, William Jennings Bryan spoke directly to his detractors and contrasted "our farms" with "your cities."

They looked only to the solutions of the past. A Populist leader, James "Cyclone" Davis, barnstormed the country, giving speeches while he kept a volume of Jefferson's complete works with him at the podium. When someone asked him a question about regulating corporations or government ownership of railroads—he would open the book and page through it, looking for the answer. The answer wasn't there.

Jefferson's vision of a democratic, equal America was being threatened because those who believed in it were just defending his methods, instead of coming up with new ways to reach his goal.

But then another group did just that. They were the progressives. Here in Oregon, they developed the "Oregon system" to take power from political machines and give it back to the people. Woodrow Wilson and Teddy Roosevelt thought of—and then Franklin Roosevelt and Harry Truman and others put in place—a new vision of government to bring American democracy into a new century.

They weren't anxious about the new industrial, national scale economy—they were excited to its power and wealth and scope to advance their goals. So they created public schools and Social Security and the GI Bill and home loans and the interstate highway program—the building blocks of a more democratic America.

America Is Changing Again

But now we all know that America is changing yet again. We're moving from cities to suburbs and exurbs, from a national economy to a global economy, from the top-down hierarchies of the industrial age to the bottom-up workplaces of the information age, from assembly lines to iPods.

Not everyone is part of that shift, but with each passing day, more and more are. And again, American democracy is at risk.

We once again have a corrupt bargain between powerful interests and pliant politicians. Energy policy is set not by citizens or their elected representatives, but behind closed doors by lobbyists and industry. Congress prohibits Medicare from negotiating for lower drug prices. The number of registered lobbyists in Washington has doubled since 2000 and the amount these lobbyists charge their clients has increased 100 percent—and those clients are getting every cent of their money's worth. You don't have to look much further than [the] headlines to see that the voice of everyday people in our government is getting drowned out by the desires of a few.

Social equality is disappearing once again, in ways unseen since the last time our economy changed, back in the Gilded Age. Thirty years ago the top 100 CEOs made 39 times the wage of the average worker. Now it is more than 1,000 times higher. And the top 1 percent holds a third of the country's net worth. . . .

Opportunity—the idea that in a democracy each person should have an equal chance at success—is also at risk. A 1978 study showed that 23 percent of the adult men born in the bottom fifth made it to the top fifth. When they did the study over again [at the end of the twentieth century], that number had dropped to 10 percent.

Class lines are becoming hardened and the avenues of democracy are being closed off. At the country's top 146 colleges, 75 percent of the students come from the top one-

The Importance of Civic Engagement

Why do we [of the American Political Science Association] believe that improving our institutions to promote robust citizen engagement is essential to American democracy? First, civic engagement enhances the quality of democratic governance. Democratic decision making requires knowledge of the interests of the people. Citizens make their preferences known through various forms of civic engagement: casting a ballot, attending a rally, writing a public official, volunteering time, or showing up at a meeting. While there surely is a role for expertise in politics and public administration, citizen input has the potential to improve the quality of public decisions by marshaling the knowledge and registering the preferences of the entire community. . . .

Second, the promise of democratic life is not simply that government by the people yields the most excellent governance. It is also—and perhaps mainly—that government is legitimate only when the people as a whole participate in their own self-rule. Insofar as important classes of citizens are considerably less active and influential than others—especially when participatory inequalities are a consequence of the design of the political system—then the reality of collective self-rule is doubtful, and the legitimacy of the political order is compromised. Democracy is supposed to represent the interests of the people as a whole, but ample evidence supports the notion that political institutions are most responsive to those who mobilize. Government "by the people, for the people" flounders when only narrow and particularistic interests are mobilized or when important sectors of the political community are left out.

Stephen Macedo et al.,
Democracy at Risk: How Political Choices Undermine
Citizen Participation and What We Can Do About It, *2005.*

fourth and only 3 percent from the bottom one-fourth. You are twenty-five times as likely to sit next to a rich student as you are a poor one. . . .

And where the richest in our country can choose their children's schools and their family doctor and how to save for their retirement, most middle class and poor Americans have little to no say on most aspects of their lives, little ability to make decisions for themselves.

The Job of Remaking Democracy

Those of us who believe in American democracy now have a choice to make—and it is just like the choice a hundred years ago. We can try to hold back change: say no to globalization or no to technology, replacing manufacturing jobs and bank tellers being replaced by ATMs.

We can spend all our energy on criticizing right wingers for their failures and their mistakes and the errors of their vision.

We can spend all our time defending what came before: saying that Social Security is all we can do when it comes to retirement instead of adding to it, that our public school system is just fine the way it is.

We can rail against change and defend all that came before, but that won't save American democracy.

Because we will end up like James "Cyclone" Davis looking through Jefferson's works to find answers to questions Jefferson couldn't imagine. . . .

[Instead] we can do in our time what they did in theirs: offer new thinking to expand American democracy. We can build on what came before us instead of letting that progress get washed away. We can reimagine a bold vision of democracy for our own time.

Woodrow Wilson said that in America, democracy was "always a-making;" a process of progress, a goal we never quite reach. It's our job to push that progress along.

Democracy as a Way of Life

Democracy can be so much more than it is today. The Information Age is fundamentally about democratization—about power to the people. Workers have more ability to make their own decisions on the job. Consumers have more choices and more ability to shape what they buy. Our challenge now is to make American democracy come alive. To use government to give power to our people. To truly tap the talents of all. To actively break down the barriers that keep people from choosing their own path. To make equality come alive again. To make democracy mean more than elections, but real self-rule.

So let's find ways to make college universal. Let's stop running our schools on a calendar set by harvest time and let's end one-size-fits-every-kid education. Let's not be anxious about globalization but excited and use America's economic strength not just to enrich a few but to lift billions out of persistent poverty. Let's open up our decision-making process so individual people and communities make decisions instead of the elected few and distant bureaucracies. This can be a moment where we make democracy not just a form of government, but a way of life.

You see, there have always been two views of American democracy. One is that the wealthy and powerful and the educated experts are better suited to making decisions for all of us and to having control. That's the view that now drives this country's policies.

Then there's the other view that power and authority and a voice should be given to the people themselves; that prosperity flows from their efforts and that they should be given government's help in taking control of their own lives.

Let's put our faith back in people.

Let's defend our progress but never be satisfied with it. . . .

"I like the dreams of the future better than the history of the past," said Jefferson. Let's go out there and dream again.

▌ *"Americans pretend to value democracy."*

American Democracy Is a Charade

Stan Moore

In the following viewpoint, Stan Moore claims that American-style democracy is a charade. Instead of promoting equality and fairness, democracy in America has been hijacked by the wealthy and powerful to further their own interests, Moore contends. He argues that the underclasses are routinely disenfranchised in elections and that poor or underprivileged people never attain significant positions in government to bring about needed change. Moore regrets the fact that most Americans blindly accept this state of affairs and have yet to overturn the system. Stan Moore is an ornithologist and environmentalist living in California.

As you read, consider the following questions:

1. According to Moore, how does American democracy compare to retail encounters in northern California?
2. What does Moore dislike about America's status as a republic?
3. What is the "absolute key" to meaningful democracy, in Moore's view?

If one enters almost any retail business in northern California, one finds trained employees who ask with seemingly great sincerity, "How are you?" The implication is given that these employees, and by extension, their companies, actually care about the welfare of the public. And the charade is carried out by the customers themselves, who routinely seem touched to have been asked about their welfare, and who invariably respond, "I'm fine, how are you?" The reality is that neither the retail employee nor the customer actually cares enough about the other's well-being enough to actually offer assistance if it was actually needed; it is just a charade. If the customer were to actually reply, "I am in deep need, will you help?" The resulting impasse would be palpable, as the questioning had no implication of actual desire to assist.

American democracy and support of democracy around the world is a charade, just like the retail encounters we see here in northern California. Americans pretend to value democracy, but when expression of democracy is suppressed in Ohio[1] by conservatives challenging voters they don't know but whose names were collected and compiled specifically to disenfranchise the poor and underclass, Americans go right along with the charade, praising democracy all along.

When state officials whose primary jobs are supposed to monitor fairness and impartiality of the electoral process, turn out to be paid partisan political operatives of one of the parties in the election, and who may even be campaign chairpersons of one of the major candidates, the American public goes right along with the charade, and the media ignores the blatant conflict of (democratic) interest.

1. Independent reports suggest that many Ohio voters were disenfranchised during the contested 2004 presidential election. Some contended that Ohio's chief elections official, J. Kenneth Blackwell, the co-chair of the George W. Bush-Dick Cheney Republican campaign in Ohio, was involved in misconduct that resulted in the disenfranchisement.

Those Who Lack Money Lack Power

The entire American system of democracy is a charade, based on governance of the masses by the wealthy elite. You don't find poor people with good ideas involved in any significant numbers in governance, because money is the root of American democracy. If you had plenty of money and bad ideas, you have a great chance of getting elected, but if you have little money and great ideas, you are "out of the loop" and have no chance of even being nominated for high office, or low office in most cases.

If America was a democracy, meaning the intent of the largest number of voters in a presidential election was the deciding factor in the election, then Al Gore would have become president in 2000, instead of George W. Bush, because Al Gore received the largest popular vote. But America is not a democracy, it is a republic, and the electoral system in America is, and always has been, designed to represent the interests of a narrow class of wealthy, land-owning, influential elites whose interests often are at odds with the interests of the public at large, and whose interests are increasingly counterproductive to the needs of both poor and middle class. Witness the intense current campaign by both parties to "reform" the American Social Security system by robbing it blind and using the assets to further enrich the wealthy.

Iraq Represents America's Disdain for Democracy

But America's disdain of democracy and the resultant charade has probably been never more painful to behold, hypocritical and dangerous as what we have seen in Iraq. We have an election administered by an occupying power (America) through a non-elected puppet government for the purpose of serving the interests of the foreign power. We have candidates whose identities and political views are kept secret from the voting public. An informed voting public is the absolute key to mean-

Soft Money Talks Loudly

If barriers to voting discourage civic participation, the insidious and growing influence of money in politics *devalues* participation as it shifts political power from the many to the few. Consider this: "soft money" donations to the 1992 presidential campaign totaled some $86 million. By 2000 soft money grew to $500 million, and spending on the 2004 presidential campaign totaled an astounding $1.7 billion. And this despite the passage in 2002 of the hard-fought McCain-Feingold campaign finance reform bill.

Sadly, it is now true that in nearly every election, the candidate who spends the most wins. Candidates often spend as much or more time raising money than they do talking with voters. And it doesn't stop once you're in office. Sitting members of the House of Representatives must raise an average of $2,000 a day from the day they take the oath of office to the next election—in competitive races, they must raise even more. The pernicious power of money in politics undermines the standing of the *citizen* as it enhances the power of the *donor*. It creates space for undue influence over policy and, of course, for impropriety, scandal, and corruption.

Stephen Heintz, "The Democracy Crisis,"
Remarks to Alliance for Children and Families
2006 National Conference, St. Louis, October 18, 2006.

ingful democracy, yet the Iraqi public was deliberately uninformed so as to prevent a truly meaningful vote. The Iraqi election was engineered to provide the appearance of meaningful democracy, while maintaining the charade. Candidates were vetted by the occupying force. Freedom of movement of the electorate was blocked by the occupying power in order to provide "security."

The Iraqi election paves the way for further serving the interests of the foreign occupying power while attempting to legitimize the occupation and usurpance of the national governance.

Amazingly, even this charade may fall apart in the foreseeable future, again because of the insistence on the interests of the occupying power. If the results of this fraudulent election bring about a new Iraq that reflects "premature" aspirations (from the point of view of the occupier) to remove the occupation force, the will of the new government will be suppressed. If the new government aspires to unite with regional Shia Muslims and form alliances with Iran's Shia government, the will of the new Iraqi government will be repressed. If the Kurds's desire for control over oil resources in Mosul gets "out of control," that democratic desire will be suppressed. Iraq's new charade of democracy will be tolerated by the foreign occupiers only as long as it suits the interests of the occupier. If it gets out of control, it will be suppressed.

Benefiting the Few at the Expense of the Many

American-style "democracy" is not what it claims to be or appears to be. The American public willingly goes along with the charade because it seems to have created a good life for them up to now. But times are changing, the "pie" of wealth to be distributed is changing shape and shrinking, and American-style democracy will change along with it because it is all designed to benefit the few at the expense of the many, and with less to go around, the many will see their share of the pie reduced, whether they like it or not.

When the charade becomes intolerable to the masses, we will find out what Americans REALLY think about democracy.

Periodical Bibliography

The following articles have been selected to supplement the diverse views presented in this chapter.

Lynne M. Adrian	"Disasters and What They Show Us About America's Values," *Chronicle of Higher Education*, October 7, 2005.
Hugh Heclo	"Is America a Christian Nation?" *Political Science Quarterly*, Spring 2007.
Tim Keane	"Redefining 'Values,'" November 9, 2004. www.democraticunderground.com.
Jim Manzi	"A More Equal Capitalism," *National Review*, February 25, 2008.
Ted Nordhaus and Michael Shellenberger	"Why Americans Vote Their Values," *Blueprint*, July 2006.
Michael Sharkey	"Where Have American Values Gone?" *Chien Kun*, August 2006.
Amy Sullivan	"Why Democrats Are Losing the Culture War," *USA Today*, October 26, 2006.
Terry Teachout	"Our Creed and Our Character," *Commentary*, July-August 2007.
Jay Tolson	"The Faith of Our Fathers," *U.S. News & World Report*, June 28, 2004.
George Vradenburg	"Dear Fellow Republicans," *Tikkun*, January-February 2008.
Jim Wallis	"A Real 'Values' Agenda," *Sojourners*, January 2008.
Curtis White	"The Spirit of Disobedience," *Harper's*, April 2006.

OPPOSING
VIEWPOINTS®
SERIES

CHAPTER 2

Are America's Values Threatened?

Chapter Preface

The Culture and Media Institute (CMI) is an organization that seeks to counter what it sees as misinformed liberal media portrayals of religious and conservative values. In 2007, CMI released the results of opinion polls regarding what Americans perceive to be the relationship between the media and the moral health of the nation. According to the survey, titled *The Media Assault on American Values*, roughly two-thirds of Americans blame news and entertainment media for the degradation of core values such as honesty and charity and, conversely, the promotion of sexual permissiveness and homosexuality.

Brian Fitzpatrick, a senior editor at CMI and the author of the survey, provided a summary of its findings, emphasizing the connection between television viewing habits and morality. Fitzpatrick explained that "light television viewers (one hour or less per evening) are more likely to attend religious services and live their lives by God's principles," whereas "the more a person watches television, the less likely he will be to accept responsibility for his own life and for his obligations to the people around him." He also noted that television seems to have a seductive effect so that the more a person watches television, the less likely he or she would agree that the media influence the nation's morals. However, the results of *The Media Assault on American Values* led Fitzpatrick to conclude that "most Americans believe the nation's morality is slipping" and that the media are condoning—if not always endorsing—a host of moral ills from promiscuity to a blatant disrespect for clergy.

Though the CMI survey does not explain how the media influence morals (it provides only statistics of what Americans perceive), faith-based organizations and media watchdog groups have latched on to the report's conclusions as testimony to the media's role in the decline of morality. Criticism of the report, however, has been rather muted. A few have argued that social problems and their correlation to the media have always been subject to "chicken and egg" analyses, making it unclear whether the media influence morality or whether shifting social ethics influence media.

In the following chapter, various conservative social critics put forth other reasons why they believe American values may be threatened in the twenty-first century. While some attribute the perceived decline in morals to changes in family values, others blame the government for eroding the ethical foundations on which the nation was supposedly built. Like the supposed threat of media, though, these assertions have not gone unchallenged. What detractors may see as the collapse of American ideals, optimists view as the broadening of liberty and other virtues that Americans hold dear.

> "For modern-day Americans, freedom is defined by the extent to which the federal government takes care of them and protects them from the vicissitudes of life."

Government Imperils Freedom

Jacob G. Hornberger

Jacob G. Hornberger is the president of the Future of Freedom Foundation, an organization that promotes individual liberty, free markets, private property, and limited government. In the following viewpoint, Hornberger states that the welfare state, devised under Franklin Roosevelt's New Deal, has deprived Americans of the benefits of free enterprise and individual liberty. Instead, the welfare-state government takes citizens' money, dispenses morality, and does its best to control the lives of all, Hornberger claims. He believes that Americans have been tricked into believing that this system actually ensures liberty and that most Americans will continue to support the system until they recognize the value of the libertarian philosophy on which the nation was founded.

Jacob G. Hornberger, "Libertarianism Is the Key to Our Future," *Freedom Daily*, 2006. Reproduced by permission.

As you read, consider the following questions:

1. What aspects of the modern welfare state were not present in Hornberger's portrait of America in 1880?

2. In the author's opinion, what political philosophy is really at work in America under the welfare state?

3. For what reasons is the war on drugs doomed to failure, according to Hornberger?

Why do I remain convinced that the American people will return to their libertarian heritage, especially given the continued trend toward socialism and interventionism in Washington, D.C.? There are three reasons: freedom, morality, and pragmatism.

Deceptive Freedom in America

Almost everyone prizes the concept of freedom. Yet relatively few people in history have realized it. Throughout recorded history, most people have had to live their entire lives under tyrannical and oppressive governments.

The big problem that Americans face is embodied in the words of the great German thinker Johann Goethe: "None are more hopelessly enslaved than those who falsely believe they are free." Americans honestly believe that, unlike most people throughout history, they are living lives of freedom. They are not aware that they are actually living lives of unreality and self-deception.

That's not to say that Americans don't value freedom. On the contrary, it is among their highest values. They sing songs praising it and often refer to past Americans who died for freedom. It's just that when it comes to their own freedom, they are living what might be called a "life of the lie"—a life of deception—a life of delusion.

This deception regarding the nature of freedom was undoubtedly one of the greatest achievements of the Franklin Roosevelt administration in the 1930s. You'll recall that

Roosevelt revolutionized American life by making the concept of the welfare state and regulated society a permanent fixture in our nation. But rather than convincing the American people of the virtues of socialism, paternalism, and government control, as other regimes in the world were doing, Roosevelt convinced Americans that their new system was, in fact, designed to save freedom and free enterprise. Americans bought the argument and ever since have lived under an oppressive economic system that they honestly, but mistakenly, believe is freedom and free enterprise.

To appreciate the stark differences between the freedom that our ancestors celebrated and what Americans today falsely celebrate as freedom, consider the following features of life in the United States in, say, 1880:

No Social Security, Medicare, Medicaid, income taxation, welfare, occupational licensure, immigration controls, travel restrictions, passports, paper money, central bank, or drug laws and few economic regulations. People were free to engage in any economic enterprise, accumulate unlimited amounts of wealth, travel and trade wherever they wanted, and do whatever they desired with their own money.

That is what was once understood to be economic liberty. That is what it once meant to be an American. That is what it once meant to be free.

The Welfare State Needs to Be Overturned

Today, Americans obviously live under a totally opposite set of political-economic principles. All of the above-mentioned programs that were absent from American life in 1880 have become part and parcel of American life today. For modern-day Americans, freedom is defined by the extent to which the federal government takes care of them and protects them from the vicissitudes of life.

What would happen if Americans were to break through and realize the truth? What would happen if they finally came to the realization that what happened during the 1930s was not simply a reform or a "saving" of America's free-enterprise system but instead an open embrace of the socialist and paternalist philosophy and ideas that were sweeping the world?

My hunch is that if Americans were to finally confront the reality of what has happened to their country, they would choose the principles of economic liberty that are their heritage rather than the socialist principles of "freedom" that were later imported to their nation. But in order to make such a conscious choice, they first have to confront the reality of what has happened to their country in the name of "saving freedom and free enterprise."

That's why our task as libertarians remains an educational one. It is a task, of course, that involves showing people the morality and virtue of economic liberty. But it also involves the much more fundamental task of showing people the true essence of individual freedom. For once a person no longer falsely believes he is free, he is faced with a choice: Should I remain the way I am, even though I now know that I am not free, or should I take whatever steps are needed to make me free?

It is, of course, impossible to predict how each person will answer that question. But the reason that governments do their best to convince people to never ask the question, especially by convincing them to falsely believe they are already free, is that there always exists the possibility that people, upon discovering the truth, will devote their time and energy to winning their freedom before they pass from this life.

Government Is Not a Moral Institution

Almost everyone places moral principles near or at the top of his scale of values. The problem we face is that most Americans honestly believe that the welfare state and regulated society are based on moral principles. This has been another grand achievement of socialists and interventionists that again reaches back to the Roosevelt administration. Having become convinced that the welfare state and controlled society reflect how good and moral they are, Americans have also become willing, albeit unwitting, accomplices in the destruction of their own freedom.

Here is the essence of the income-tax/welfare-state argument with respect to morality:

Your American ancestors believed in a system in which everyone kept his own money and decided what to do with it. That system of rugged individualism was bad. That system failed, partly because individuals cannot be trusted to handle their own resources or to help those in need. Here is how we saved America's free enterprise system. Everyone was required to send a certain part of his income to the federal government. Democratically elected federal officials decided the percentage and each year everyone was required to send in "his share." Then federal officials disbursed the funds to the poor and needy. Along with the members of Congress, the IRS [Internal Revenue Service], and federal welfare agencies, the American people are considered good and moral as the welfare-state disbursements are made.

Here is the controlled-society argument with respect to morality:

Your American ancestors didn't believe in drug laws, which means that they favored the use of harmful substances. Many of them abused their freedom by ingesting alcohol, cocaine, marijuana, and other harmful drugs. To do such things to one's body is immoral. The federal government, consisting of democratically elected public officials, used the power of the government to stamp out such immorality. By refraining from doing something immoral, even if out of fear of state prosecution and punishment, the American people are now more moral as a result.

What would happen if Americans were to discover that the welfare state and controlled society actually violate prin-

Laws Should Safeguard Personal Rights

People should have the freedom to act according to their desires, but only to the extent that they do not trample on the rights of others. Rules and regulations, such as traffic laws, need to be established and enforced by private and public institutions in order for a free society to exist. There should be stringent laws against fraud, theft, murder, pollution, and the breaking of contracts, and those laws should be effectively enforced according to the classic principle that the punishment should fit the crime. The full weight of the law should be used to line and imprison the perpetrators, to compensate the victims, and to safeguard the rights of the innocent. Yet within this legal framework, we should permit the maximum degree of freedom in allowing people to choose what they think, act and do to themselves without harming others.

Mark Skousen, "Persuasion Versus Force,"
Advocates for Self-Government, 1992. http://theadvocates.org.

ciples of morality? What would happen if they came to the realization that it is morally wrong to take a person's money from him by force, even if the money is going to be spent for a worthwhile cause? What if people came to the realization that it is morally wrong for the state to punish a person for making bad or sinful choices that inflict no violence on another person? What if they realized that moral principles dictate that individual persons be free to make such decisions for themselves, even if the results are not to the liking of others in society?

My hunch is that if Americans were to come to grips with the real moral implications of the welfare state and regulated society, they would turn to economic liberty and libertarianism. But in order to do that, they must first realize that they must make a choice—a choice between the immorality of the welfare state and controlled economy, and the moral principles that underlie the genuinely free society. As long as they continue to remain mired in the false reality that the welfare state and regulated society reflect people's moral goodness, they have no need to consider the libertarian alternative.

Socialism Is Defective

It would be virtually impossible to find any aspect of the socialistic welfare state and controlled society that works—that is, that achieves the declared ends of those who support such programs.

Consider some of the major crises that confront our country: Social Security, Medicare, Medicaid, the dollar, Iraq, terrorism, immigration, the drug war, and education.

Do you notice a common denominator in all these programs? The federal government! The federal government has made a mess out of all of these areas of life. (Of course, the disaster of public schooling is rooted in socialist education at the local level, but certainly federal officials have made the situation worse with their subsidies, interventions, and controls.)

These disastrous results are not surprising to libertarians. Why? Because we have long known that socialism cannot work. It is incapable of working, even when the planning and regulating is done by U.S. bureaucrats. Socialism is inherently defective, as the people of the Soviet Union finally realized. But the difference is that they, unlike Americans, understood that theirs was a socialist system. What Americans still do not realize is that no matter how hard they try, they will never make any of their socialist programs succeed. And the primary reason they don't understand that is that they think that their system is freedom and free enterprise, which they rightly understand do succeed.

Controls Cannot Staunch a Free Market

Consider, for example, the drug war. No matter how much the government cracks down—mandatory minimum sentences, asset forfeiture, extraditions of foreign drug lords, violations of financial privacy, chemical spraying of drug crops, infringements of civil liberties—it will never succeed in ending drug use or drug abuse.

Why is this so? Because the participants in a free market (which becomes the "black market" when the activity is made illegal) will always figure out ways to circumvent the laws. Crack down on cocaine, and the free-market price of cocaine goes up. When the price goes up, that attracts new suppliers. New suppliers mean more cocaine will be available for sale.

Consider, as another example, the decades-long war on immigrants. No matter how many reforms have been enacted in the last several decades to stem the tide of illegal aliens into the country, such reforms have not succeeded. One of the most important of the reforms was the one that criminalized the hiring of illegal aliens, which supporters said would finally resolve the problem because there would no longer be jobs available to the immigrants. Now, 10 million illegal aliens later, some members of Congress are suggesting that enacting new criminal penalties—this time on Christian church groups that assist illegal aliens—will finally stem the tide of illegal immigrants.

But immigration controls will never work. Why? Because they are nothing more than socialist central planning, a process that is inherently defective. Just as in the Soviet Union, government officials are trying to plan a vast labor market which involves millions of people, each of whom is making his own decisions on the basis of constantly changing market conditions.

I repeat: No matter what government officials do—no matter what new reforms are enacted—the drug war will fail and the war on immigrants will fail. The same holds true for

Social Security, Medicare, Medicaid, public schooling, and all the other socialist and interventionist programs that afflict our society.

This point deserves constant emphasis and reemphasis. The reason is obvious: Once Americans finally come to the realization that no matter what is done with these programs, they're going to fail anyway, then why would they continue supporting calls for new reforms? Why continue engaging in an act of futility? What would be the point of continuing to waste so much time and energy when one knows in advance that the result is doomed?

Returning to Libertarianism

So why do Americans continue to look for that ideal reform that will finally bring success to America's socialist programs? Because they don't recognize these programs as socialist! They think that the programs are "free-enterprise." And they think that the programs are moral because they're intended to help people.

That's why freedom, morality, and pragmatism are inexorably intertwined. Once Americans break through to the truth and realize the true socialist nature of their economic system—and its immoral premises—they will more easily understand why all these programs have failed and will continue to fail no matter what is done to reform or save them.

Once that breakthrough and realization take place, there is but one alternative for the American people to turn to: freedom and the free market—economic liberty. In a word, libertarianism.

Libertarianism, not socialism or interventionism, is the cornerstone of our nation's heritage of freedom. Libertarianism succeeds in producing rising standards of living, nurtures voluntary charity, and promotes harmonies among people. It is a philosophy grounded in the moral foundations of freedom. Libertarianism is the key to the future of our nation.

"Experience gives us no reason to conclude that government is the only, or always the gravest, threat to freedom."

Government Can Expand Freedom

William A. Galston

Libertarians hold that any government restrictions upon individual freedoms are not in accord with America's founding principles. William A. Galston argues in the following viewpoint that this notion is flawed. He maintains that the government has often used its power to curtail liberty to promote the common good. For example, he points out that the purpose of Social Security taxes was to compel Americans to contribute a portion of their income to provide a safety net for all citizens once they have reached retirement age. Thus, the limiting of personal choice, Galston contends, benefits society as a whole. William A. Galston is a professor at the University of Maryland's School of Public Policy.

As you read, consider the following questions:

1. According to Galston, what institutions do conservatives expect will create a virtuous citizenry in lieu of government involvement?

William A. Galston, "Taking Liberty: Liberals Ignore and Conservatives Misunderstand America's Guiding Value: Freedom," *Washington Monthly*, April 2005. Reproduced by permission.

2. Why does Galston say that freedom in the abstract does not exist?

3. How does Galston use the right to assistance of counsel during trials as an example that supports his thesis?

A t a 1956 conference, [economist] Milton Friedman argued that a free market was the necessary foundation for societies in which individual liberty flourishes. What had begun as the precondition of freedom soon became its template: Libertarian conservatives redefined freedom as the right to choose and extended this understanding far beyond the market, to social relations and public policy.

These thinkers encountered a challenge within the emerging conservative movement, from traditionalists who focused on values such as order and virtue and who questioned the social consequences of the unfettered market. This tension was not in all respects an outright contradiction and thus proved to be manageable. In his classic *Capitalism and Freedom*, Friedman acknowledged that every form of social organization—including the market—relies on a framework of generally accepted rules, and that "no set of rules can prevail unless most participants most of the time conform to them without external sanctions." Not only must participants internalize rules, he continued, they must also develop certain traits of character. These requirements are especially demanding in systems of liberty: Freedom can be preserved, he concluded, "only for people who are willing to practice self-denial, for otherwise freedom degenerates into license and irresponsibility."

Arguments for Free Market Society

This line of argument raised a key question: If virtue was needed for a free society, and if we are not born virtuous, how are we to acquire it? Here entered the second premise of modern American conservatism, the proposition that civil society will generate a virtuous citizenry if only government leaves it alone to do its vital work. Not government, but rather families, neighborhoods, and faith communities sustain the moral foundations of freedom. This conservative synthesis of markets and civil society, which suffused Ronald Reagan's first successful presidential campaign, achieved lapidary statement in George W. Bush's second inaugural. "In America's ideal of freedom," he declared, "the public interest depends on private character—on integrity and tolerance toward others and the rule of conscience in our own lives. Self-government relies, in the end, on the governing of the self. That edifice of character is built in families, supported by communities with standards, and sustained in our national life by the truths of Sinai, the Sermon on the Mount, the words of the Koran and the varied faiths of our people."

President Bush's reference to the Sermon on the Mount reminds us that synthesizing the market and civil society does not fully resolve the tension between libertarians and traditionalists. After all, it was on that occasion that Jesus advised his listeners not to heap up earthly treasure because no one can pursue more than one master: "You cannot serve God and mammon." At this point, the third premise of contemporary conservatism comes to the rescue. This is the thesis, developed by American Enterprise Institute scholar Michael Novak, among others, that capitalist markets, far from undermining individual virtues and social bonds, actually fortify them. Capitalism, Novak insists, both depends upon and builds virtues such as initiative, enterprise, and social cooperation. A government that minimizes the appropriation of wealth for public purposes maximizes the scope for acts of Christian charity. And more than that: Life in capitalist societies promotes the highest form of freedom—namely, the creativity of the human person. There are also echoes of this argument in President Bush's second inaugural, especially when he claimed that moving from social provision to individual ownership strengthens individuals' moral capacities to meet the "challenges of life in a free society."

This is, let us admit, a powerful and evocative conception of freedom, blending a constellation of ideas with deep resonance in American culture. It serves, moreover, as the basis of a powerful coalition between economic interests seeking less regulation and lower taxes and moral traditionalists disturbed by the cultural changes of the past forty years. Whether we think of ourselves as progressives, liberals, or New Democrats, we cannot evade the challenge posed by these ideas and by the political currents they have set in motion. If we do not meet them head-on, we will prevail only infrequently and accidentally. And when we lose, which will be most of time, we will deserve it.

Undermining the Libertarian View

There will be a temptation by many, especially on the left, to think that this fight can be won merely by "reframing" the debate—that is, using the word "freedom" to shift the discussion to other philosophical terrain, like economic fairness and social justice, on which today's left is more comfortable. That temptation should be avoided. Because freedom has its own context and logic, we cannot make it mean whatever we like. As the great British philosopher of freedom Isaiah Berlin reminds us, "Everything is what it is: liberty is liberty, not equality or fairness or justice." When conservatives promote their tax and fiscal policies as advancing economic freedom, liberals cannot expect to get very far by complaining endlessly that such policies are "unfair." They certainly are, and more scrupulous leaders would be ashamed to propose them. But if we have learned anything since the collapse of the liberal hegemony in the 1960s, it is that the appeal to freedom trumps the appeal to fairness.

Instead of dodging the issue, an effective center-left strategy should begin with a critique of the fundamental conservative conception of freedom because that conception is fatally flawed. Experience gives us no reason to conclude that government is the only, or always the gravest, threat to freedom; clerical institutions and concentrations of unchecked economic power have often vied for that dubious honor. Nor has the ideological synthesis of markets and civil society abolished the very real problem at issue between libertarians and traditionalists: The unchecked market regularly produces social outcomes at odds with the moral conditions of a free society. Thus, it is that a conservative FCC [Federal Communications Commission] chairman pledged to media deregulation ends up imposing new restraints in the name of decency. Nor is it easy to believe that capitalism reliably produces, or rewards, the good character a free society needs: Perceptive observers from Charles Dickens to Tom Wolfe have given us ample evidence to the contrary. And while it may be that long-term dependence on government saps the spirit of self-reliance that liberty requires, there are other forms of dependence—economic, social, and even familial—that can, and often do, damage character in much the same way.

Public Power Can Advance Freedom

At the heart of the conservative misunderstanding of liberty is the presumption that government and individual freedom are fundamentally at odds. At the heart of any liberal counteroffensive must be a subtler but more truthful proposition: Public power can advance freedom as well as thwart it.

In the real world, which so many conservatives steadfastly refuse to face, there is no such thing as freedom in the abstract. There are only specific freedoms, which differ in their conditions and consequences. FDR [Franklin Delano Roosevelt] famously enumerated four such freedoms, dividing them into two pairs: freedom of speech and worship; freedom from want and fear. The first pair had long been recognized and enshrined in the Constitution. The second were a new formulation, and Roosevelt made them concrete when he signed Social Security into law, justifying it as a way of promoting freedom from want: "We have tried to frame a law which will give some measure of protection to the average citizen and to his family . . . against poverty-ridden old age." Three years later, he declared that Social Security payments will "furnish that minimum necessity to keep a foothold; and that is the kind of protection Americans want."

The conservatives of Roosevelt's era disparaged the second pair as "New Deal freedoms" rather than "American freedoms," as do many conservatives today. But those who have experienced the freedoms made possible by the New Deal are not so dismissive. It is often observed, rightly, that Social Security has virtually eliminated poverty among the elderly. But this noble achievement has an equally profound flip side. Throughout human history, those who reached the age where they could no longer work have typically depended on their children or on charity for their basic subsistence. Social Security broke this age-old dependency by giving the elderly a minimum degree of economic self-sufficiency. It is almost impossible to exaggerate how much this independence means to seniors. It is why Social Security has become the third rail of American politics. Seniors react with ferocity to efforts to "reform" the program not merely because they are defending a source of income, but because they are defending their freedom.

Liberals seldom talk about Social Security or other programs in terms of freedom. But they should. George W. Bush certainly does. In his second inaugural address, Bush accepted the validity of Roosevelt's concept of Four Freedoms. But he went on to contend that in today's circumstances, his brand of conservatism—his so-called "ownership society"—offers more effective means to traditional New Deal ends: "By making every citizen an agent of his or her own destiny, we will give our fellow Americans greater freedom from want and fear." [Bush proposed the implementation of personal retirement accounts through which citizens could opt out of collective Social Security to save for their own retirement in individual accounts.] In essence, the president was saying that his solution to Social Security's fiscal problems would provide seniors with the freedom from want and fear they had come to expect, but with two additional liberties: freedom of choice, and freedom from government dependence.

Eroding Freedom from Want

On the face of it, this is a very appealing promise. But as a matter of actual policy, it is a deeply dishonest one. Allowing individuals to invest a portion of their payroll taxes in the stock market necessarily exposes those individuals to greater financial risk, and therefore, puts their freedom from want at risk. Yet any attempt to minimize those risks—by having the government pick which funds individuals can invest in, or requiring the annuitization of those investments upon retirement, as the president has suggested—necessarily erodes the freedom of choice and freedom from government control that are the selling points of private accounts. Indeed, the more conservatives add such risk-minimizing features to their proposals to mollify the public's legitimate fears that they may be left penniless in their old age, the more those proposals will come to resemble the traditional Social Security program that conservatives are trying to escape.

The president's promises are unsound not just on the level of policy, but on that of principle. "Freedom of" and "freedom from" have distinctly different structures and implications. "Freedom of" points toward spheres of action in which individuals make choices—for example, which faith to embrace, or whether to embrace any faith at all. The task of government is to secure those spheres against interference by individuals, groups, or government itself. By contrast, "freedom from" points toward circumstances that (it is presumed) all

Government Improves American Life

It is not an exaggeration to say that a good portion of the improvement in the quality of Americans' lives during the last 100 years has been due to the efforts of our federal, state, and local governments. Consider, for instance, the wide variety of vital roles and functions that big government plays in our society. Things like providing roads and sewers and other essential infrastructure facilities, preventing economic depressions, eliminating horrible diseases like polio and smallpox, ensuring drinkable water and breathable air, dispensing justice, providing retirement security, preventing business abuses, sponsoring stunning scientific breakthroughs, feeding the hungry, recalling unsafe products, educating our children, reducing workplace injuries and deaths, responding to disasters and emergencies, preventing crime, protecting civil liberties, rescuing endangered species, ensuring the safety of drugs, guarding our national security, caring for the elderly, and so on.

Seen this way, it is clear that the supportive role that government plays in all our lives is indispensable. We are usually told that the high quality of life enjoyed by so many people in the United States is due to the abundance created in the private sector, but in fact it is also due to the many activities of the public sector. The good life as we know it in the United States literally could not exist without the constant assistance and protection we all get from an extensive network of government laws and programs. Efforts by anti-government politicians to drastically cut taxes and reduce government programs are putting this good life in jeopardy.

Douglas J. Amy, "Government Is Good: An Unapologetic Defense of a Vital Institution," 2007. www.governmentisgood.com.

wish to avoid. In such instances, the task of government is, so far as possible, to immunize individuals against undesired circumstances. Here government acts to protect not individual agency and choice, but rather individuals' life-circumstances against outcomes that no one would choose, or willingly endure. We do not suppose, for instance, that slavery is a matter of individual choice; rather, after much struggle, we have come to a collective decision that no one in his right mind would prefer slavery to freedom, and we have ordered our laws and institutions accordingly. Similarly, during the New Deal, we made a collective decision that no senior would willingly live in penury and shouldn't have to.

Limiting Some Freedoms to Promote Others

It follows that libertarian freedom, the "right to choose," is but a part of freedom in the fuller sense. As a motorist, I am rightly free to choose my own route and destination. But government correctly infers that I also wish to be protected from smashing into other cars, and so restricts which side of the road others and I may drive on. My desire to avoid an accident is no less real than my desire to drive where I please. Similarly, the desire to avoid want and fear is no less real than the desire to speak and worship without interference. The point is that any society that takes freedom from want and fear seriously has made a collective decision: Certain conditions are objectively bad; its citizens should not have to endure them if the means of their abatement are in hand; and individual choice is not a necessary component of and may be a hindrance to attaining these freedoms.

In addition to presuming that freedom must always involve individual choice, conservatives tend to mischaracterize and misunderstand many aspects of freedom, in particular, its costs. Freedom from want and fear often requires citizens to contribute some of their individual resources for collective purposes and makes better-off citizens contribute more. Conservatives have a tendency to focus on these costs without factoring in the benefits, and thus they often do not see or acknowledge that the net result is an increase in freedom. It has often been observed, for instance, that freedom for the pike is death for the minnow. Curtailing the freedom of the pike is often the only way of securing the freedom of the minnow. And there are usually far more minnows than pikes. So when government leans against the depredations of the powerful, it is enhancing freedom, not curtailing it. When government acts to ward off, or break up, excessive concentrations of private power, it does not diminish, but rather enhances, liberty rightly understood.

Freedom for Many Benefits Society

Specific freedoms often have conditions for their effective exercise, and government must sometimes act to ensure broad access to those conditions. A familiar but not trivial example: Nothing safeguards liberty more than the rule of law; fair trials are essential to the rule of law; and the Sixth Amendment's guarantee of the "assistance of counsel" for every accused is essential to fair trials. Many Americans cannot afford to pay for defense lawyers, and the legal profession does not contribute enough pro bono hours to fill the gap. The government, therefore, taxes better-off Americans to provide legal counsel for the disadvantaged. In the process, it unavoidably restricts individuals' freedom to use those tax dollars for other purposes. But does anyone seriously doubt that this use of government's taxing power enhances the sum of freedom in our country?

Another example: Under modern conditions, the freedom of individuals to participate in the labor market requires the mastery of work-related knowledge and skills, many of which can only be acquired through formal education. The government uses its power of taxation to ensure that this education is within the reach of all families regardless of their private resources. While this policy restricts the ability of wealthier families to use those tax dollars for private purposes, the overall result is to advance freedom within the wider society.

| *"The lust for money, dominance, and military power is at the core of America's moral decline."*

Money and Power Are Eroding American Values

Karen Horst Cobb

Karen Horst Cobb, a journalist and artist, claims in the following viewpoint that many Christian leaders promote capitalism as a moral philosophy. Horst Cobb states that high-profile evangelists are acquiring huge fortunes by marketing products to their followers. With money comes power, and Horst Cobb fears that wealthy Christian lobbies are now supporting unchristian policies such as military dominance and war in the Middle East. Horst Cobb insists that church leaders return to preaching compassion and peace to staunch the moral decline that has resulted from the lust for money and power.

As you read, consider the following questions:

1. According to Horst Cobb, how do capitalist Christians compare to infomercial spokespersons promoting real estate schemes?

2. As the author states, how many people does the Christians United for Israel lobby reportedly represent?

3. What complaint does Horst Cobb have against John Hagee's book *Jerusalem Countdown*?

"This is the year God wants to make you a millionaire." The visiting evangelist stomped back and forth on the stage of the rented school building. His "hallelujahs" and "praise God" crescendos were followed by jumping up and down. Sweat ran down his face as he proclaimed that the church members would not need to be afraid if the economy collapses and their neighbors' houses are foreclosed upon because they are blessed and will have all of their needs met. The service ended with the explanation that the first step to becoming a millionaire is to pledge $200 of "seed faith money" to the church.

Just prior to the introduction of the evangelist, the young single minister with spiky hair introduced the beginning of fellowship "life groups," explaining that the "free market" will decide which ones succeed. Recently, Ted Haggard of megachurch New Life Fellowship in Colorado Springs explained that Spirituality is a "commodity" to be bought and sold. The writings of [free market economist] Milton Friedman are recommended for all new converts. This young minister must also be a free market convert. His small group is a satellite of World Harvest Church. The sermon themes of the megachurches are all very similar and reflect the cause of America's moral decline. Christianity is getting a makeover using the classic trappings of money, domination and military aggression.

Christian Capitalism

It looks like the 50 million dollar Bible theme park which was to be built in Israel by evangelicals will not happen now that [evangelist] Pat Robertson insulted [former Israeli prime minister] Ariel Sharon. Imagine a 50 million dollar Bible theme park protected by nuclear weapons in the holy land and off limits to Arabs. The harvest of the megachurch is ready; welcome the gleaners, the seed faith money has matured.

According to a 2003 article in *Forbes* magazine, big churches are big business. Researchers found that in 2003 there were 740 megachurches each averaging 6,876 participants. The average net income of each was $4.8 million at the time of the study. The *Forbes* article states, "[the] entrepreneurial approach has contributed to the explosive growth of megachurches."

Is it the entrepreneurial spirit or the Holy Spirit which is enticing the converts to this new religion? Some used to say that the love of money is the root of all evil and the rich man (like the camel) will forever be outside the kingdom. I guess that is just "too first century" for the modern believer. The millennium church makeover is all about Christian capitalism, he whom the free market has set free shall be free indeed! Remember, this is the year God wants me to be a millionaire.

Some might think that putting your last hundred bucks in the offering satchel as "seed faith money" is a lot like gambling or buying a lottery ticket. Perhaps [chairman of Focus on the Family] James Dobson and Ralph Reed can explain that to the Indians. (and the rest of us.) A *Washington Post* article explains that Ralph Reed (former head of the Christian coalition) "received $4 million to whip up public sentiment against expansion of gambling in Louisiana and Texas." He did this by mobilizing evangelicals to take a stand against the immorality of gambling.

Wealth Leads to Power

The buildings and technologies of the megafellowships are edifices to capitalism, free market economics, and the entrepreneurial spirit. The lexicon is slightly different but the concepts are exactly the same as those of CEO motivational speakers or a slick late night infomercial promoting real estate schemes. You can do it! You can win! You can be a success!

The Megachurch Experience

It looks like a mall on a busy holiday weekend, but it is the Willow Creek Community Church, and it could be any weekend. In almost every city or suburb of more than 200,000 there is a similar megachurch, as they are known, a product of suburban sprawl, religious marketing, consumer demand, the entertainment economy, and the good old-fashioned yearning for communal experience. Megachurches draw young, committed, and energetic members; listen to parishioners talk and you will hear a refrain of growth— "we're growing"—as if it were proof of redemptive success. And they deliver a highly emotional product: the marriage of group affiliation and a conversion experience, complete with videos, pop music, and other modern dramatic flourishes.

James B. Twitchell, Mother Jones, *March-April 2005.*

You are smart! There are no limits to what you can achieve. Just send me some money and get started today. A quick Internet search reveals sources concerning the personal lifestyles of the pastors of many of these churches. Their seed faith has been harvested into private jets, extravagant cars, multimillion dollar homes and much, much more. The storehouses are overflowing and with this wealth comes power.

Like Ted Haggard's New Life Fellowship in Colorado Springs, World Harvest Church is a very politically active megachurch. Rod Parsley is the pastor, "co-laborer," as he puts it. He is also founder and president of the politically active "Center for Moral Clarity." In a few weeks he is scheduled to speak on the topic "the War on Christians and the Values Voter in 2006" at the Vision America Conference. Other speakers scheduled for the event are Alan Keyes, Senator Sam Brownback, John Comyn, Gary Bauer, Phyllis Schlafly, Janet Parshall, Rick Scarbrough, and Tom Delay. (Yes that's right— the multiply-indicted Tom Delay.)

I have not listened to Pastor Parsley's CD set "Injustice in American Courts" nor have I purchased the shiny "King Arthur style sword" for $41.10 to display in my home. I have not considered taking courses at World Harvest Bible College where I can learn to "shape the culture" nor have I spent the thousands necessary to learn how to "walk in *Dominion power* to advance the kingdom of God through the earth" [italics added].

In his Ohio community, religious leaders exposed the use of Pastor Parsley's religious tax-free status to support Gubernatorial candidate Ken Blackwell. Yes, the same Ken Blackwell who was the cochair of the committee to re-elect Bush/Cheney in 2004 while at the same time responsible for overseeing Ohio's election which ended up with many irregularities.

Parsley and Blackwell launched a voter registration campaign but only to register Republican voters. Money leads to power and power leads to war.

The Christian War Lobby

It seems today there is a need for a tougher, meaner Jesus, a government issue Jesus (GI-Joe) who comes complete with state of the art Kevlar tunic, two edged sword, and secret code book (the book of Revelation). Evangelical Christians are organizing and conspiring to manipulate governments to use weapons if necessary to kill some of God's children so that prime real estate goes to people whom they believe God likes best.

This immoral clarity was reported recently in the *Jerusalem Post*. Rev. John Hagee is the organizer and leader of the Armageddon war cry and has now created the powerful political lobby, Christians United for Israel (CUFI). Christians United for Israel (CUFI) includes Jerry Falwell, Benny Hinn,

Jack Hayford, George Morrison, Rod Parsley and Steven Strang and many other media evangelicals. According to Hagee, "The goal is to be strategically placed to successfully lobby Washington on behalf of Israel ... Every state in the Union, every congressional district will be accounted for." Reportedly, this lobbying group represents 30 million evangelical Christians. As we know, Congress alone has the power to declare war. Will it be Christians who pressure elected officials into war? Will it be people who declare themselves to be Christ-like, who use his name to sound the collective war cry which unleashes the deadliest weapons on earth? George W. Bush said recently that "all options are on the table" when it comes to Iran.

The Evangelical Christian right is working to ensure a manmade apocalypse develops in the Middle East. This powerful political faction runs parallel to the economic foreign policies of the slightly more secular neo-conservative "Republican" party which has visions of empire and military rule as outlined in the Project for a New American Century's "Rebuilding America's Defenses: Strategies, Forces And Resources For A New Century." It was written a year before 9/11, and, prophetically, the plan to put bases throughout the Middle East is right on schedule. John Hagee's latest book is *Jerusalem Countdown* which can be viewed on his Web site. Evidently, it presents Iran as a horrible nuclear threat to Israel and the United States. Just for a quick check with reality here is the score on nuclear weapons: Iran–0, Israel–200, US–10,600 (as of 2002). Please explain to me who are these "people of faith" and what do they put their faith in? Experts agree that Iran is at the very least ten years away from obtaining even one nuclear warhead. Ten years is a lot of time to wage peace.

Loss of Compassion for Others

Theocratic capitalism appeals to human lust for money, power, and military rule. Conversely, simplicity, service, and humility belong to the divine. Confusing fables are taught to itching ears. (Timothy 4:3 paraphrased). The first century followers of Christ did not entertain the entrepreneurial spirit, market competition and accumulation of wealth or organized to lobby Caesar.

For some, generosity is a strategy to gain wealth to purchase political power. Christ-like generosity however results from empathic compassion and a longing for the welfare of others. This is the core of moral clarity and makes it impossible for true believers to horde wealth. The rich man and the camel are both unable to kneel low enough to pass through the eye of the needle. (Matthew 19:24).

In the upside down kingdom Jesus taught that the poor are rich, the weak are strong, and the servant is the master. It is a change of heart rather than a change of legislation and circumstances. The new Jerusalem is a community governed by the golden rule, not ancient real estate governed by religious politicians. A person living in love does not need Power-Point seminars, CD boxed millennium sets, ornamental swords, or novels written in code. It's all summed up in a sentence and a sacrifice—Love the lord and love your neighbor.

Warriors lust for more powerful weapons. If the Christians United for Israel are successful in lobbying Washington on behalf of Israel they will ensure that more living souls will be destroyed. God is not an angry real estate broker who uses extortion and violence to get his way. He does not think of suffering and dying children as "collateral damage."

America's Moral Decline

The charred bodies in Fallujah [Iraq] incinerated by white phosphorus were living souls. Deformed babies fused together or born without limbs because of the use of depleted uranium weapons is beyond depravity. It is estimated that 150,000 living souls have been extinguished directly or indirectly as a result of the war in Iraq. Many of these are women and children.

Beautiful news models and impressive military strategists describe "magnificent" weapons and manipulate us into pride and patriotism brought to us by companies with military contracts. With deadened empathy we watched the "shock and awe" as whole families explode before our eyes. What families' values support this behavior? The American dilemma remains unspoken. If I become aware, how can I remain comfortable and keep shopping?

The lust for money, dominance, and military power is at the core of America's moral decline. It is imperative that church leaders and laity boldly proclaim that violence, torture, hostage taking, conquests of land and resources are actions Christians can never condone. Killing for Christ is an abomination leaving us with blood-stained hands and darkness in our hearts! Every church must be a peace church or it will become a state church and then it will be . . . no church at all.

> *"Any parent so irresponsible as to fail to demand chores and a work ethic from young children is asking for trouble."*

Young Americans Need a Stronger Work Ethic

Ted Nugent

In the following viewpoint, musician and television show host Ted Nugent registers his disdain for America's young people who lack a strong work ethic. According to Nugent, in decades past, children learned self-reliance and the value of work; today, he bemoans, parents pamper and spoil young Americans because they believe that hard work might hurt their children's "feelings." Nugent attests that teaching children independence is good for them and good for American society.

As you read, consider the following questions:

1. What kinds of jobs did Nugent have by age twelve?

2. Why do parents keep their children from working, according to Nugent?

3. In Nugent's argument, why do some Americans believe that immigration is desirable?

Ted Nugent, "Cultivating Work Ethic Is Vital for Children, for America," *Waco Tribune-Herald*, July 22, 2007. Reproduced by permission of the author.

The New York journalist, and I use the term "journalist" generously, was attempting to take me to task for claiming that slovenliness and laziness are unnecessary choices anywhere, anytime, but especially in America.

I had just explained to him how, as a child of a lower middle-class family living on the outskirts of Detroit in the roaring 1950s, I got nothing unless I earned it.

We did without. We were frugal by design. You want a guitar, kid? Get a job. Or two.

I went into detail how my mother and father loved me and properly parented us kids in the most powerful and positive of ways by teaching us real-world self-esteem as something that only comes from genuine effort, sacrifice and intelligent, conscientious prioritization.

By age twelve, I had two paper routes, washed cars, swept sidewalks and driveways, sold night crawlers, shoveled snow, raked leaves, cleaned eaves, painted fences, mowed lawns, trimmed hedges, cleaned windows and performed a myriad of other work duties beyond my routine household chores.

It was expected in my family. I took pride in earning my keep and contributing to the family asset column.

Pampering a Generation

Plan B is for the Osbournes and Paris Hiltons of the chump world.

Sad, really.

The reporter scoffed that such opportunities were somehow not realistic in America, 2007.

With a smarmy sarcasm, he chuckled, "catching and selling night crawlers? Do you actually believe that is a realistic opportunity for kids today?"

Well, not if the little brats are catered to, cleaned up after and provided with every electronic gadget, superfluous clothing of trendy choice and bling-bling to choke a welfare goat without a hint of effort, no.

Young Workers' Sense of Entitlement

Once hired, young people too often come in on Day One wanting to be vice president but not wanting to pay the dues to get there. They want to know what the company is going to do for them, and they rarely think about what they intend to do for the company. In fact, the whole notion of working often seems like an inconvenience.

Ruben Navarrette,
Union-Tribune *(San Diego), July 8, 2007.*

Such entrepreneurial creativity as mine certainly would be camouflaged by the feel-good fog of denial and cult of crybaby prima donna whiners. You know who they are.

God forbid little Johnny or Suzie might get his or her lily-white, manicured, dainty hands dirty. That might embarrass them and hurt their feelings and self-esteem.

I got news for ya, Bubba. Any kid who doesn't have daily chores has yet to feel honestly good about himself. Any parent so irresponsible as to fail to demand chores and a work ethic from young children is asking for trouble.

That parent is helping to create a spineless, tragically dependent America. I, for one, would like to thank you for nothing.

Opportunities Are Everywhere

I look around me every day across this amazing country, and my eyes see more opportunities for creative, driven young Americans than one could possibly take advantage of.

I see trash everywhere that quality businesses would love to pay someone to clean up. I see filthy windows and unkempt yards that a few bucks here and there to a good, hard-working, responsible kid would go a long, long way to up-grade.

I see dirty cars, dilapidated fences, broken signs, burnt-out lights, wrecked kennels.

I see piles and piles of recyclable debris that a thoughtful person or small business would gladly pay for removal and re-cycling. I see it everywhere.

I keep hearing how illegal immigration is OK and even desirable but for the lie that "Americans refuse to do those jobs." Really?

If we reward people for sitting around picking their noses and twiddling their thumbs, it is no surprise that we have ac-tually trained people to be dependent instead of productive, happy, fulfilled citizens.

Shame on us. Shame on them.

Teach Children Independence

Digging ditches, picking crops and doing hard labor is not something to be avoided or ashamed of.

Just the opposite. Sitting around letting others take care of you is surely the worst, soulless condition known to mankind. It is clearly a self-inflicted form of slavery, and I don't like it.

Kids are desperately seeking action, challenge, guidance, prodding, discipline. (Haven't we heard this somewhere before?)

Don't cater to them. Don't pick up after them. Put them to work.

Teach them the wonderful sensation of productivity. Fan the flames of independence and teamwork while celebrating rugged individualism. They will love you for it, and it is your job. Make them do theirs.

| *"Thrift is still the essential virtue that makes the American dream possible."*

Americans Should Relearn the Value of Thrift

Ray Boshara and Phillip Longman

Ray Boshara is the vice president of the New America Foundation, a public policy institute. Phillip Longman is a senior fellow at the New America Foundation. In the following viewpoint, the two authors claim that America has forsaken the value of thrift and built up a hefty consumer and government debt. With prices of many commodities on the rise, Boshara and Longman suggest that Americans re-embrace thrift—the wise allocation of money—to avoid financial tragedy. The authors also contend that government and lending institutions could bolster Americans' attempts to save by implementing frugal policies and rewarding those who follow them.

As you read, consider the following questions:

1. According to Boshara and Longman, how much disposable household income goes toward non-mortgage debt repayment?

Ray Boshara and Phillip Longman, "Forget Easy Money. Try Saving a Few Bucks," *Washington Post*, October 7, 2007, p. B03. Copyright © The Washington Post Company. Reproduced by permission of the authors.

2. As Boshara and Longman state, in what way did thrift once equate with conservation?

3. What kinds of socially desirable behaviors do the authors suggest could be rewarded by governments, civic-minded corporations, and philanthropists through deposits into consumer savings accounts?

Countrywide Financial, the nation's largest mortgage lender, has a curious new idea—or, more precisely, an old one. No longer will it use wads of Chinese cash recycled through Wall Street to make subprime loans to unqualified borrowers. Instead, it will take in deposits from small savers and lend them out to people who might actually repay them—just like that humble thrift institution president George Bailey did in *It's a Wonderful Life.*

Imagine: a bank that promotes thrift! This could be the start of something big. Writing recently in the *American Banker*, Eugene Ludwig, a former comptroller of the currency, advised financial institutions to stop relying "on the easy money that comes from wholesale funding" and to concentrate instead "on harder-to-get core deposits." How quaint. Remember when banks actually tried to instill the savings habit by going into schools and helping kids set up small passbook accounts? Today, the first experience most younger Americans have with a bank comes during freshman orientation at college, when they come across a table laden with giveaways and credit-card applications.

America's Financial Crisis

This return to thrift comes none too soon. Not since the Great Depression have so many Americans lost their homes in one year—and we're not even in a recession, at least not yet. But we're still on course to see 2 million foreclosures in 2007, afflicting one in 62 households. That's a 67 percent increase from 2006, according to Realty Trac. The Federal Reserve's recent decision to cut its benchmark rate by half a point, while widely praised on Wall Street, will do little to stop the slide.

Also not since the Great Depression have Americans saved so little. Even with unemployment at historically low levels, Americans spent more than they earned in both 2005 and 2006—and charged the difference. Household debt, not including mortgages, now eats up nearly 15 percent of disposable income—more than food and gasoline combined. One in seven families is dealing with a debt collector. Children today are more likely to live through their parents' bankruptcy than their parents' divorce. Americans' stunning lack of savings not only brings personal tragedy but also is causing the dollar to plummet against all major currencies, jeopardizing our economic growth and threatening the financial system worldwide.

Prices Are Going Up

What's going on? No doubt, some of us like to shop too much, but it's also true that the "fixed costs" of middle-class life have soared. Elizabeth Warren, a professor at Harvard Law School, shows that while family incomes have gone up in the past generation, the costs of health care, education, housing, child care and transportation have risen even higher.

Meanwhile, not only does the government itself borrow as though there were no tomorrow, primarily through unfunded health and pension plans, but it promotes what David Blankenhorn of the Institute for American Values calls "anti-thrift" institutions. Today, 41 states plus the District of Columbia and Puerto Rico run lotteries, and 11 states encourage casinos. Government has also allowed for the mainstreaming of other anti-thrift institutions—some charging annual interest of more than 500 percent—that once existed, if at all, only in the shadows of society. Payday lenders, rent-to-own stores, auto-title lenders, some franchise tax preparers and chain pawn shops are all now as common across the landscape of middle-class America as Applebee's.

After the terrorist attacks of 2001, President Bush told us that the patriotic thing to do was to shop. But Osama bin Laden is still out there, gas is more expensive than ever, the credit card is maxed out and our homes are depreciating. There's a better way: the old-fashioned virtue called thrift.

The Wise Use of Money

Historically, thrift didn't carry its current association of being cheap or stingy. Rather, it meant the wise use of resources. It meant an abhorrence of waste, whether of raw materials, time, energy or money. In short, it meant conservation.

To conserve money, working-class men and women banded together to create "thrift" institutions. Before these institutions were deregulated and taken over by the fast-buck crowd in the 1980s, they provided a staid but reliable vehicle for building a nation of "freeholding" middle-class homeowners and small-scale entrepreneurs. Most Americans understood, until the triumph of the anti-thrift institutions, that their own freedom from wage slavery—and, indeed, the civic health and wealth of the republic—depended on the savings habit and the widespread ownership of unencumbered small properties that it makes possible.

Today, by contrast, while many Americans understand the need to conserve energy and natural resources, they have trouble seeing what any of that has to do with credit cards and subprime mortgages. But conserving financial resources is not only still essential to individual liberty; it is also essential to moderating wasteful consumption and saving the environment.

Reviving the American thrift ethos won't be easy, and it will probably take at least a generation. But we can take some small steps now that would make saving easy, automatic and frequent. Our goal should be to generate new savers as well as new savings—in sharp contrast to current government policy,

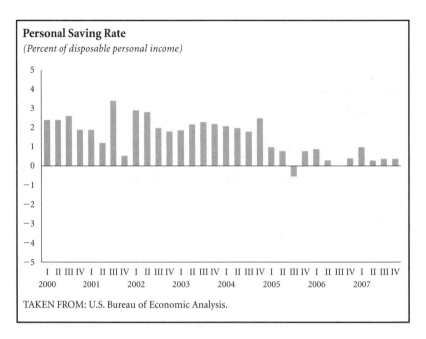

Personal Saving Rate
(Percent of disposable personal income)

TAKEN FROM: U.S. Bureau of Economic Analysis.

which allocates considerably more than $100 billion a year in tax breaks to high-income earners who would save anyway.

What Government and Financial Institutions Could Do to Promote Saving

First, we should take advantage of one of the most powerful forces *in* human nature: inertia. Studies in behavioral economics show that when new hires have to opt *out* of a 401(k) retirement plan, as opposed to having to opt in, savings rates skyrocket. Also, building on the "Opportunity NYC" initiative (which is being privately funded by the Rockefeller Foundation, New York Mayor Michael R. Bloomberg and several other donors), governments, civic-minded corporations and philanthropies could make automatic savings deposits to individuals who engage in socially desirable behavior. Finish high school, volunteer in your community or buy an energy-efficient appliance, and your savings account receives a deposit.

Technology, if fully exploited, can also make the cost of maintaining a bank account far lower, thereby giving financial institutions a greater incentive to serve small savers and giving freedom to the "unbanked" poor from the gouging fees that payday lenders charge to cash checks. Imagine that your debit card is also an interest-paying savings card, to which your employer, the Internal Revenue Service and other entities can make automatic deposits. Some innovative firms are already offering such a product, which combines low cost with convenience and security.

Meanwhile, regulators should encourage more community-focused banks, credit unions and thrift institutions. These can resume their historical role of promoting thrift by helping customers become savers as well as (eventually) homeowners and small-business owners.

Congress should do its part as well. The bipartisan New Savers Act, for example, makes it easier to open bank accounts, buy savings bonds, put money away for college and receive financial education. Another bipartisan measure, the Automatic IRA Act, encourages automatic payroll deposits into IRAs. Other proposals authorize tax credits for low-income savers, as well as remove savings penalties for those on public assistance.

Finally, to usher in this "new thrift" across generations, Congress should establish a lifelong savings account for all children when they are born—a reality in Britain and elsewhere and an idea that's rapidly gaining bipartisan momentum in the United States.

Thrift Is an American Value

If you're an American born in the twentieth century, thrift probably strikes you as a musty, downscale word—reminiscent of used clothes, aged relatives who wrapped their sofas in plastic or perhaps the grandmother who saved Green Stamps. But it's worth remembering, as did generations of Americans struggling up from poverty and privation, that thrift is still the essential virtue that makes the American dream possible.

Periodical Bibliography

The following articles have been selected to supplement the diverse views presented in this chapter.

America	"The True Costs of War," May 15, 2006.
Benjamin R. Barber	"The Lost Art of Cooperation," *Wilson Quarterly*, Autumn 2007.
William Bole	"Want to Stay Married?" *Commonweal*, July 16, 2004.
Heather Boushey	"Values Begin at Home, but Whose Home?" *American Prospect*, March 2007.
Sam Brownback	"A Family Crisis," *New York Times*, March 2, 2008.
Midge Decter	"Stop Compromising on 'Civil Unions,'" *USA Today*, March 2007.
Tim Dickinson	"The Politics of Fear," *Rolling Stone*, June 29, 2006.
Kay S. Hymowitz	"Gay Marriage vs. American Marriage," *City Journal*, Summer 2004. www.city-journal.org.
Peter Wehner and Yuval Levin	"Crime, Drugs, Welfare—and Other Good News," *Commentary*, December 2007.
Patrick Welsh	"For Once, Blame the Student," *USA Today*, March 8, 2006.
Mortimer B. Zuckerman	"Our Cheating Hearts," *U.S. News & World Report*, November 6, 2006.

OPPOSING
VIEWPOINTS®
SERIES

CHAPTER 3

How Should Patriotism Be Defined?

Chapter Preface

In a July 2005 issue of *Blueprint* magazine, Will Marshall, president of the Progressive Policy Institute, asserts that "Since 9/11, patriotism has become the most potent 'values issue' in U.S. politics." Indeed, a scant forty-five days after the terrorist attacks in New York, Pennsylvania, and Washington, D.C., President George W. Bush and a mostly receptive Congress passed the Uniting and Strengthening America by Providing Appropriate Tools Required to Intercept and Obstruct Terrorism (USA PATRIOT) Act, a piece of legislation giving law enforcement agencies unprecedented powers to search personal records and monitor telephone and e-mail communications of American citizens suspected of having connections to terrorists or their plots. Those who support this act believe that every American has a duty to ensure that another tragedy does not befall the nation; those who oppose it contend that surrendering the right to privacy should not be equated with patriotism. This division has also been evident in subsequent debates over other aspects of the war on terror, including, most prominently, the 2003 invasion of Iraq—a nation that the Bush administration argued was developing weapons of mass destruction and trafficking with America's terrorist enemies.

Critics of unquestioning allegiance to the government's pursuit of the war on terror insist that laws like the USA PATRIOT Act and acts of aggression overseas reveal the dark side of patriotism. While most Americans love their country and would defend it in a crisis, those who question blind adherence to the state suggest that citizens are often trading liberties for the increased power of government. In a 2002 essay for anti-state.com, writer Gus Ellis argues that "patriotism simply cannot see beyond the state." He maintains that the American Revolution was fought against tyranny to uphold the freedom of the individual. Since then, however, Ellis contends that American patriotism has betrayed "the better values of the American Revolution by celebrating the state and condoning power."

Writer and poet Colleen Redman believes that the questioning of the state—especially in its pursuit of the war in Iraq—may signal a return to the patriotism espoused by the colonial revolutionaries. "Perhaps the substantial protest of Americans from all walks of life is a sign that a new sense of patriotism is being reborn, the kind reminiscent of our Founding Fathers, who also challenged the status quo and who bravely fought against the abuse of imperialistic power," Redman suggests. She further testifies, "I am greatly inspired by those who have publicly spoken out against our actions in Iraq, despite the risk that they will probably be mocked and discredited. Those who have done so have caused me to broaden my understanding of the meaning of patriotism and have made me want to be a more informed and active citizen."

Many of the viewpoints in the following chapter support Ellis's and Redman's arguments. Jonathan M. Hansen, for example, insists that dissent is a form of patriotism when people use it to further equality and the rule of law not only at home but also in America's foreign policy. As other commentators in the chapter make clear, however, not everyone equates the right to dissent with a duty to dissent. Conservative spokespersons point out that dissent invites division, often hamstringing the nation when military action is needed to ensure the safety of the United States. They maintain that patriotism implies a unified support for government action during crises that threaten national security. The following viewpoints exemplify this ongoing debate, revealing how different Americans define the value of patriotism in the post-9/11 world.

| "Any American who stands against patriotism stands against American values."

American Nationalism Is a Force of Good

Ben Shapiro

In the following viewpoint, Ben Shapiro argues that liberals are wrong to blame much of the world's misfortune on American nationalism. Unlike other forms of nationalism that have in the past sown seeds of evil, American nationalism is based on positive virtues. According to Shapiro, the world has benefited from the spread of democracy and other values that American nationalism has inspired. Ben Shapiro is a law school graduate and the author of Porn Generation: How Social Liberalism Is Corrupting Our Future.

As you read, consider the following questions:

1. As Shapiro reports, who said "Patriotism is the last refuge of a scoundrel?"

2. According to Shapiro, why is nationalism itself not an evil?

Ben Shapiro, "In Defense of Patriotism," *Creators Syndicate* (Creators.com), July 11, 2007. Copyright © 2007 Creators Syndicate, Inc. By permission 'author's name for text entries' and Creators Syndicate, Inc.

3. On what criteria do American values discriminate, in Shapiro's view?

The American left is fond of bumper sticker slogans. One of their favorites comes from arch-wit Samuel Johnson, who once reportedly remarked, "Patriotism is that last refuge of a scoundrel." Johnson was describing false patriots—his 1755 dictionary defined "patriot" as "one whose ruling passion is the love of his country." Nonetheless, leftists have rallied around the antipatriotic banner.

Their current leader is lauded scholar and campus hero Professor Howard Zinn, quasi-Marxist author of the virulently anti-American *A People's History of the United States*. On July 4, Zinn posted his most recent diatribe against patriotism: "On this July 4, we would do well to renounce nationalism and all its symbols: its flags, its pledges of allegiance, its anthems, its insistence in song that God must single out America to be blessed." He wrote, "We need to refute the idea that our nation is different from, morally superior to, the other imperial powers of world history. We need to assert our allegiance to the human race, and not to any one nation."

Blaming America

Zinn's point of view is radically blunt, but it is a mainstream component of American liberal thought. According to the left, the current chaos in Iraq is a result of American arrogance rather than religious sectarianism; America's failure to embrace European relativism must be attributed to a benighted American exceptionalism.

Blaming the world's ills on American nationalism is a predictable result of a broader attempt to undermine nationalism. Nationalism, in this view, inherently carries with it a pernicious distinction between "us" and "them"—a distinction that often leads to dehumanization and human rights abuses. Hannah Arendt articulately summed up the sentiment: "I have

American Patriots Are Tolerant Until Provoked

American patriots appreciate just how lucky they are to live in this country. They understand how many people sacrificed everything to get us to this point, and how many more sacrifices will have to be made to keep us here. True patriots don't go around telling people from other countries how superior Americans are to them. They don't hate anybody who hasn't exhibited a hatred for America first, and they're perfectly willing to let other countries be, just as long as they don't threaten America's interests.

Patriotic Americans also understand that you can't build up your country if you spend all your time trying to tear it down, and I've yet to meet a liberal who hasn't attempted to wreck some aspect of American culture at some point in their lives.

Edward Daley, "In Defense of Patriotism,"
Conservative Voice, *May 12, 2005. www.theconservativevoice.com.*

never in my life 'loved' any people or collective—neither the German people, nor the French, nor the American, nor the working class or anything of that sort. I indeed love 'only' my friends and the only kind of love I know of and believe in is the love of persons."

This critique carries a grain of truth. Nationalism clearly creates distinctions—those within the nation are more highly prized than those outside it; national goals are more important than the goals of outsiders. And in many cases, these inherent traits of nationalism cause more harm than good. Nazi Germany's nationalism meant Holocaust and fascist conquest; Soviet Russia's nationalism meant purges of dissidents and tyrannical expansionism.

American Nationalism Is Based on Respectable Virtues

Nationalism, then, reflects the values of the nation. For some nations, nationalism *is* an evil. But it is an evil not because nationalism is inherently evil—it is an evil because the national values manifest in that particular brand of nationalism are themselves evil. A nation that seeks evil is evil; a nation that seeks good is good. The problem isn't nations—the problem is values.

And not all values are equal. Those who oppose patriotism on its own terms either embrace the lowest sort of moral relativism or foolishly bank on a set of yet-to-be-discovered universally accepted values.

American patriotism does indeed create outsiders and insiders, as all value systems do. But the distinctions drawn in America are based on the highest set of values ever embodied in national form. American values discriminate based on hard work, determination, individual initiative and traditional moral values. They do not discriminate based on race, religion, class or sex.

American patriotism is the deeply held belief and hope that American values ought to be purveyed—that the spread of American values is good for humanity. Any American who stands against patriotism stands against American values—the same values responsible for the liberation of Europe, the end of Soviet communism, the spread of democracy around the globe and the most tolerant society ever devised.

"Is not nationalism—that devotion to a flag, an anthem, a boundary so fierce it engenders mass murder—one of the great evils of our time, along with racism, along with religious hatred?" Zinn asks. Not American nationalism, untold millions answer. God blesses America uniquely because America blesses the world uniquely. Anti-Americanism is the last refuge of the fool; American patriotism is the sanctuary of the good.

"In a nation like ours ... what might have been harmless pride becomes an arrogant nationalism dangerous to others and to ourselves."

American Nationalism Is a Force of Evil

Howard Zinn

Howard Zinn is a well-known political scientist and social critic. In the following viewpoint, Zinn insists that American nationalism has led most Americans to believe that their country is superior to others in the world. This, he argues, has fostered a sense that America has a mission to spread its style of liberty and democracy around the globe. Unfortunately, in Zinn's view, American nationalism has produced much brutality as the country has often sought to impose its values through wars and other imperialistic means. Zinn advocates that Americans renounce nationalism and view themselves as global citizens.

As you read, consider the following questions:

1. How does Zinn define nationalism?

2. What is the earliest example of destructive American nationalism to which Zinn refers in his viewpoint?

3. In Zinn's view, what is the lie that the government tells American soldiers today?

On this July 4 [2006], we would do well to renounce nationalism and all its symbols: its flags, its pledges of allegiance, its anthems, its insistence in song that God must single out America to be blessed.

Is not nationalism—that devotion to a flag, an anthem, a boundary so fierce it engenders mass murder—one of the great evils of our time, along with racism, along with religious hatred?

These ways of thinking—cultivated, nurtured, indoctrinated from childhood on—have been useful to those in power, and deadly for those out of power.

National spirit can be benign in a country that is small and lacking both in military power and a hunger for expansion (Switzerland, Norway, Costa Rica and many more). But in a nation like ours—huge, possessing thousands of weapons of mass destruction—what might have been harmless pride becomes an arrogant nationalism dangerous to others and to ourselves.

American Exceptionalism Is Self-Deception

Our citizenry has been brought up to see our nation as different from others, an exception in the world, uniquely moral, expanding into other lands in order to bring civilization, liberty, democracy.

That self-deception started early.

When the first English settlers moved into Indian land in Massachusetts Bay and were resisted, the violence escalated into war with the Pequot Indians. The killing of Indians was seen as approved by God, the taking of land as commanded by the Bible. The Puritans cited one of the Psalms, which says: "Ask of me, and I shall give thee, the heathen for thine inheritance, and the uttermost parts of the Earth for thy possession."

The Threat of Ideological Patriotism

It is . . . important to recognize that any ideology, no matter how admirable at its outset, can be captured and subverted; and moreover, to recognize that when thus subverted it is very likely that those inebriated by it, and thus committed to its propagation, will not recover from their stupor, but will rather fall deeper into its narcotic effect. In short, a successful ideology will breed suspect interests all around it.

In sum, we live in a dangerously ideological age. In our own lifetimes, millions have perished at the hands of ideologists. Prudence counsels that we make our most resolute effort, not to reform the ideologies that swirl menacingly around, but to protect the good things of our inheritance from that threatening cloud.

Paul J. Cella and Jeff Martin,
"Patriotisms: True and False," What's Wrong with the World,
June 6, 2007. www.whatswrongwiththeworld.net.

When the English set fire to a Pequot village and massacred men, women and children, the Puritan theologian Cotton Mather said: "It was supposed that no less than 600 Pequot souls were brought down to hell that day."

On the eve of the Mexican War, an American journalist declared it our "Manifest Destiny to overspread the continent allotted by Providence." After the invasion of Mexico began, the *New York Herald* announced: "We believe it is a part of our destiny to civilize that beautiful country."

The Liberty and Democracy Myth

It was always supposedly for benign purposes that our country went to war.

We invaded Cuba in 1898 to liberate the Cubans, and went to war in the Philippines shortly after, as President McKinley put it, "to civilize and Christianize" the Filipino people.

As our armies were committing massacres in the Philippines (at least 600,000 Filipinos died in a few years of conflict), Elihu Root, our secretary of war, was saying: "The American soldier is different from all other soldiers of all other countries since the war began. He is the advance guard of liberty and justice, of law and order, and of peace and happiness."

We see in Iraq that our soldiers are not different. They have, perhaps against their better nature, killed thousands of Iraq civilians. And some soldiers have shown themselves capable of brutality, of torture.

Yet they are victims, too, of our government's lies.

How many times have we heard President [George W.] Bush and Secretary of Defense Donald Rumsfeld tell the troops that if they die, if they return without arms or legs, or blinded, it is for "liberty," for "democracy"?

Americans Must See Themselves as Citizens of the World

One of the effects of nationalist thinking is a loss of a sense of proportion. The killing of 2,300 people at Pearl Harbor becomes the justification for killing 240,000 in Hiroshima and Nagasaki. The killing of 3,000 people on Sept. 11 becomes the justification for killing tens of thousands of people in Afghanistan and Iraq.

And nationalism is given a special virulence when it is said to be blessed by Providence. Today we have a president, invading two countries in four years, who announced on the campaign trail [in 2005] that God speaks through him.

We need to refute the idea that our nation is different from, morally superior to, the other imperial powers of world history.

We need to assert our allegiance to the human race, and not to any one nation.

"There is nothing more patriotic . . . than defending liberty and equality at home and human rights and the rule of law around the world."

Dissent Is Patriotic

Jonathan M. Hansen

Author of The Lost Promise of Patriotism: Debating American Identity, 1890–1920, *Jonathan M. Hansen is a historian who, in the following viewpoint, defends dissent as a form of patriotism. In Hansen's view, after the September 11, 2001, terrorist attacks on the United States, American patriotism was synonymous with unquestioned support for retaliation and war in Iraq. Instead, Hansen argues that liberal dissenters who disapproved of war and advocated the deliberate pursuit of equality and the rule of law were the true patriots. In his opinion, and the opinion of the liberal dissenters, national loyalty was not opposed to global justice and the peaceful fostering of democratic ideals worldwide.*

As you read, consider the following questions:

1. What three groups of liberal dissenters were smeared as unpatriotic after the September 11, 2001, attacks, in Hansen's view?

Jonathan M. Hansen, "Liberal Dissenters Are Patriots, Too," *History News Network* (hnn.us), October 13, 2003. Reproduced by permission.

2. As Hansen explains, what did liberal patriots argue was the best way to ensure genuine and lasting solidarity on the American home front after the terrorist attacks?

3. According to Hansen, why is dissent not corrosive to the morale of American troops in battle?

In the immediate aftermath of 9/11 [2001], the United States experienced a spontaneous and nearly universal ground-swell of patriotism. For many liberals the feeling of solidarity with the nation as a whole came as a surprise. Having ceded patriotism to conservatives since the Vietnam War, liberals had little sympathy for patriotism's emotional force and no sense of its potential usefulness. But on 9/11 the nation was attacked by an enemy that did not discriminate on the basis of gender, class, color, or, ironically, creed. In response, Americans united, pledging part of their fortunes and, in some cases, their lives to succor the victims and vanquish the perpetrators.

Wielding Patriotism Like a Truncheon

In the ensuing weeks and months, as shock and grief gave way to blame, the fellow-feeling eroded and patriotism became re-politicized. The first to be smeared by the epithet "un-patriotic" were those whose understanding of the deep seated, historically rooted antipathy to American power around the world did not permit them to absolve the United States of all responsibility for terrorism. Next came those who saw the solution to terrorism not in a leaner, meaner American military galvanized around preventive strikes, but in a foreign policy less solicitous of autocrats and more aware of global suffering. Then came those who, in the build up to the Iraq war, thought the U.S. government should abide by international law. Conservatives, incidentally, were not the only ones to impugn skeptics' patriotism; self-described progressive "hawks" proved no less ready to wield patriotism like a truncheon.

And so, from a liberal perspective, by April 2003, things looked pretty much the way they looked back in the late 1960s: citizens who opposed the war and questioned administration policy were tarred with treason and effectively silenced, as dissent became, once more, un-American. What is to be done?

Defending Equality and the Rule of Law

Liberals could be excused for once again surrendering patriotism to the Super Patriots. But, intriguingly, many seem reluctant to do so, as if the experience of 9/11 has heightened their appreciation of the value and vulnerability of American institutions. This inclination ought to be encouraged. Not only would American democracy benefit from vigorous dissent undertaken in the name of patriotism, but liberal politics would acquire the rhetorical amplitude it so conspicuously lacks. There is nothing more patriotic, after all, than defending liberty and equality at home and human rights and the rule of law around the world.

Although it is seldom acknowledged today, this was the position of many Progressive-Era intellectuals and social critics, whose attempt to redeem patriotism from jingoism a century ago should interest contemporary liberals. With America facing foreign and domestic challenges strikingly similar to our own, the philosopher William James, the settlement house leader Jane Addams, the socialist agitator Eugene V. Debs, the civil-rights advocate W.E.B. DuBois, and the future Supreme Court Justice Louis Brandeis, among a host of others, propounded a vision of patriotism rooted in liberal democratic principles and committed to constant, critical civic vigilance. The principal opposition of their liberal patriotism, as we might call it, was not between American and outside interests, as now seems to be the case, but between equality and justice, on the one hand, and racism, sexism, industrial exploitation, and imperialism, on the other.

Reclaiming Moral Authority

I believe ... that the best way to support the troops is to oppose a course that squanders their lives, dishonors their sacrifice, and disserves our people and our principles. When brave patriots suffer and die on the altar of stubborn pride, because of the incompetence and self-deception of mere politicians, then the only patriotic choice is to reclaim the moral authority misused by those entrusted with high office.

I believe ... that it is profoundly wrong to think that fighting for your country overseas and fighting for your country's ideals at home are contradictory or even separate duties. They are, in fact, two sides of the very same patriotic coin.

John Kerry, "Dissent,"
Remark delivered at Faneuil Hall,
April 22, 2006.

The Work of Liberal Patriots

On the home front, the liberal patriots argued that the way to ensure genuine and lasting solidarity was not to intimidate immigrants and political dissenters but to demonstrate the salience of the nation-state—i.e., the federal government—to the well-being of all Americans: *E Pluribus Unum* meet *Quid Pro Quo*. The liberal patriots were not jealous sentinels of the people's hearts. They did not regard local loyalties (whether ethnic, racial, regional, or religious) as anathema to national loyalty, or national loyalty, in turn, as inimical to global allegiances. Citizens first learn about loyalty at the local level, they recognized; without local education in obligation, national loyalty would be impossible.

The liberal patriots were devoted to America's founding principles, but they saw no reason why those principles could not extend over the entire earth. They viewed democracy as a universal impulse, but they did not construe the U.S. Constitution as the final word on democratic governance. They regarded as compatriots individuals of any nation who shared their commitment to liberal democracy, just as they denounced individuals, institutions, and governments—at home and abroad—that compromised that fundamental ideal. The liberal patriots expected American foreign policy to uphold the democratic ideals regulating life inside the Republic. For a nation founded upon putative universal values, promoting those values universally constituted the ultimate form of self-defense.

Supporting the Troops

Here, surely, was a vision of patriotism appropriate for a culturally dynamic society in a fluid, globalizing age. It is one contemporary liberals could be proud of. But before liberals can adopt such patriotism, they will need to demonstrate the courage of their conviction by staking out discursive ground. One place to begin is by demolishing once and for all the shibboleth that political dissent is somehow corrosive to the morale of American troops—an argument that is always the last refuge of entrenched political elites. Not only does this argument slight the professionalism of our troops—if they can't stomach political controversy at home, how will they endure the vicissitudes of war?—but it leaves the fate of the troops, like the policy that deployed them, in the hands of a tiny minority: the president and the department of defense. Were I a private in the U.S. Army, I'd want the whole country seriously invested in my fate.

Nothing could be more supportive of American troops—indeed, of America itself—than citizens keeping a critical eye on the political justifiability and moral rectitude of the nation's cause. In the absence of such critical vigilance, the soldier's valor, like patriotism itself, becomes arbitrary.

| "[Dissent] is the opposite of courage—it
| is the height of conformity."

Dissent Is Not Patriotic

Aryeh Spero

Rabbi Aryeh Spero hosts a radio talk show and is the president of the Caucus for America, a conservative organization that lobbies to preserve American values. In the following viewpoint, Spero lashes out at liberal dissenters, claiming that those who seek only to criticize the nation are cowards. Spero insists that dissenters are leftist snobs who avoid military service and work to undermine the security of the country by stripping it of its defenses.

As you read, consider the following questions:

1. According to Spero, how do liberal elitists view military service?

2. In Spero's view, what leads liberal dissenters to loathe the military?

3. Why does Spero believe liberal dissent is a "class thing?"

With fewer liberals than ever enlisting in our armed services or serving in command positions, liberals have redefined patriotism to mean "dissent," protesting against U.S.

Aryeh Spero, "Patriotism Means Service, Not 'Dissent'," January 9, 2006. www.human events.com. Reproduced by permission.

policy. Why? Because that is what liberals do. They criticize their country and moralize to their countrymen. They are generally not policemen, firemen or soldiers. They are "above" the rest of us.

But dissent is not service. Dissent is simply personal gratification, a right guaranteed. Though I have a right to eat, my eating is not an act of patriotism. Patriotism is service; and the act of denouncing one's country simply serves one's personal need to be heard.

Likewise, idealism has been redefined by many liberals to mean doing that which undermines U.S. attempts at self-defense and condemning one's country abroad, even though by so doing one jeopardizes the physical safety of fellow citizens.

Dissent Is Liberal Conformity

More often than not, left-wing parents of these "idealistic" young people are far more proud of their children engaged in "dissent" than if they were serving in the military. To these elitists, military service is an embarrassment, beneath their class, a sign of failure to have really "achieved." But such is the luxury of certain well-heeled, comfortable, haughty elements in our society. They can confer upon themselves and their dissent the label "courage" knowing that other peoples' 19- and 20-year-olds are out there making sure that they, the perpetual protestors, are safe to vent their disdain for this country, our safety, and the military protecting them.

In fact, it is the opposite of courage—it is the height of conformity. For in their circles, dissenters against everything American are lauded and praised as sophisticated, cosmopolitan, smarter. Dissenters are not parochial but internationalists, i.e., better.

In today's politically-correct milieu, the truly courageous are those willing to buck the salon mentality by being pro-American.

Dissent Carries a Measure of Accountability

The right to dissent ... is part of what makes America great (but far from the only thing). That right carries with it a duty of responsibility and a measure of accountability, such as incurring the scorn of the many who do love this country. You may dissent to your heart's content, but the substance of your statements will not be exempted from scrutiny merely because you are exercising rights we consider sacred in America.

David Limbaugh, "Dissent Does Not Equal Patriotism,"
WorldNet Daily, *March 14, 2003. www.worldnetdaily.com.*

Painting Military Service as Ignoble

One would have hoped the sophisticates could at least have given the military its due, a grateful recognition. Instead, this clique of "patriots" does whatever it can to stymie the military and even denigrates our soldiers' backgrounds. New York City media elites and their neighbors tell us that our soldiers are uneducated, rednecks, that they come from the poorer regions of the country and enlist, therefore, not out of a sense of duty and honor but out of a need to have a job and make some money.

By disallowing R.O.T.C. [Reserve Officials' Training Corps] on campus and harassing military recruitment officers, they send their personal message that military service is ignoble and those that serve are engaged in something bad. By being ever so eager to indict our soldiers for war crimes whenever a quick decision is needed to save a U.S. life over that of a terrorist, it is obvious they care not a wit about our young heroes, wishing instead to demonize them.

That many seem indifferent to our soldiers is a consequence of their not having, today, family, friends or neighbors in the military. Many do not personally know an active marine or army gunner. It is true that soldiers do not pass the "interesting" test that has now become the standard for admiration within fashionable social circles. After all, it is not as if a soldier were a wealthy anti-American novelist, or an engaged gay couple, or Tookie Williams [co-founder of the Los Angeles Crips gang].

Yet, to have such rage at those things military and at our soldiers implies more than simply ignorance or a difference in opinion. It has to be personal. The antagonism is so emotional! What is behind, as one famous liberal said, this loathing of the military?

Criticism Hides Cowardice and Jealousy

It is jealousy and bitterness. Jealous that with all their education and sense of betterness, they do not have the courage to do what the soldier does. Though not afraid of the courtroom, they are afraid of the battlefield. They are better at appeasement and words than hand-to-hand physical combat. They could not live the Spartan soldier life, nor rely on a gun for survival.

Many of us cannot soldier, but we have the grace and humility to be grateful to those who can. There is, however, a certain type of liberal that will not abide in others the masculinity he can not muster—a masculinity that he was taught, early on, to fear and, therefore, despise.

It is a meanness: "I will not credit that which I've chosen—out of fear—not to do. I will not acknowledge that which reflects, deep down, my weakness." They deny their weakness by depicting the army as an evil war machine unworthy of them and conceal their selfishness by claiming those who serve do so not out of honor and duty but as a means for temporary employment.

Turning Values Upside Down

Leftists are bitter that instead of our country relying on them, the schooled internationalists, to negotiate our outcomes, we as a country place our hope in the strength of our military and soldiers to achieve victory and, thereby, determine our destiny. "How dare George Bush overlook the negotiating, Jaw-Boning Class—the 'best and the brightest'—and place our future in the hands of generals and those Ollie North [a lieutenant colonel known for stalwartly defending his part in the secret Iran-Contra dealings in the 1980s] types. Why, most of them never went to Columbia or Brown, as did we."

Yes, it is a "class" thing. Today's liberal leaders, and most of their children, are snobs. They are convinced they are superior. They've become rich, and smug. Imbued with this "appreciation" of themselves, they gravitate to the political philosophy that, today, thinks in condescending terms, a nouveau class-ism where the "enlightened" are supposed to rule and get all the credit—not the military.

Back in the 1960s, the left derided values like patriotism and heroism. They scoffed at these antiquated, bourgeois, puritan notions. I remember. I was there. Living now in an age where steadfast values have resurfaced, the liberal/left imputes them to itself. In its Orwellian way, it has turned core values upside down to match what it is: Patriotism is dissent, heroism is making your country defenseless. Soldiers are misfits, and those like the President wishing to protect our children, are a threat to our security.

Are these people evil or misguided beyond hope? Perhaps, they are simply immersed in a spoiled world with no relation to reality or history. Beyond question, they are wound up in an arrogant sense of superiority over their countrymen. I don't think America has ever been plagued by an educated, wealthy group so ardently un-American. How did it come about that America bred in its midst such self-worshipping ingrates and self-centered brats?

> *"How can it be said that blind support for war, no matter how misdirected the policy, is the duty of the patriot?"*

True Patriots Resist Unconscionable Wars

Ron Paul

In the following viewpoint, Ron Paul, a Republican member of the U.S. House of Representatives, refutes the notion that patriotism implies blind acceptance of government-sponsored warfare. In Paul's opinion, true patriots are those who resist unconscionable government actions, including wars that force citizens to trade liberties for increased state power. Ron Paul represents the Fourteenth Congressional District of Texas and ran as a Republican candidate for the 2008 presidential election.

As you read, consider the following questions:

1. What motivates the true patriot, in Paul's view?

2. According to Paul, what is the best way for Americans to show their support for the nation's military troops?

3. In Paul's opinion, why do governments find it useful and convenient to engage in multiple, ongoing wars?

Ron Paul, "In the Name of Patriotism (Who Are The Patriots?)," May 22, 2007. www.house.gov/paul.

For some, patriotism is "the last refuge of a scoundrel." For others, it means dissent against a government's abuse of the people's rights.

I have never met a politician in Washington, or any American for that matter, who chose to be called "unpatriotic." Nor have I met anyone who did not believe he wholeheartedly supported our troops wherever they may be.

What I have heard all too frequently from various individuals is sharp accusations that because their political opponents disagree with them on the need for foreign military entanglements, they were "unpatriotic, un-American, evildoers deserving contempt."

Resisting Abusive Government

The original American patriots were those individuals brave enough to resist with force the oppressive power of King George. I accept the definition of patriotism as that effort to resist oppressive state power. The true patriot is motivated by a sense of responsibility, and out of self interest—for himself, his family, and the future of his country—to resist government abuse of power. He rejects the notion that patriotism means obedience to the state.

Resistance need not be violent, but the civil disobedience that might be required involves confrontation with the state and invites possible imprisonment.

Peaceful non-violent revolutions against tyranny have been every bit as successful as those involving military confrontation. Mahatma Gandhi and Dr. Martin Luther King, Jr. achieved great political successes by practicing non-violence, yet they themselves suffered physically at the hands of the state.

But whether the resistance against government tyrants is non-violent or physically violent, the effort to overthrow state oppression qualifies as true patriotism.

True patriotism today has gotten a bad name—at least from the government and the press. Those who now challenge the unconstitutional methods of imposing an income tax on us, or force us to use a monetary system designed to serve the rich at the expense of the poor, are routinely condemned. These American patriots are sadly looked down upon by many. They are never praised as champions of liberty as Gandhi and Martin Luther King Jr. have been.

Liberals, who withhold their taxes as a protest against war, are vilified as well—especially by conservative statists.

Patriotism Is Not Blind Support for War

Unquestioned loyalty to the state is especially demanded in times of war. Lack of support for a war policy is said to be unpatriotic. Arguments against a particular policy that endorses a war once it's started, are always said to be endangering the troops in the field. This, they blatantly claim, is unpatriotic and all dissent must stop. Yet it is dissent from government policies that defines the true patriot and champion of liberty.

It is conveniently ignored that the only authentic way to best support the troops is to keep them out of dangerous, undeclared, no-win wars that are politically inspired. Sending troops off to war for reasons that are not truly related to national security—and for that matter may even damage our security—is hardly a way to "patriotically" support the troops.

Who are the true patriots: those who conform or those who protest against wars without purpose? How can it be said that blind support for war, no matter how misdirected the policy, is the duty of the patriot?

[Early twentieth-century writer and progressive thinker] Randolph Bourne said that "war is the health of the state." With war, he argued, the state thrives. Those who believe in the powerful state see war as an opportunity. Those who mistrust the people and the market for solving problems have no trouble promoting a "war psychology" to justify the expansive role of the state.

This includes the role the federal government plays in our personal lives as well as in all our economic transactions. And certainly the neo-conservative belief that we have a moral obligation to spread American values worldwide, through force, justifies the conditions of war in order to rally support at home for the heavy hand of government. It is through this policy, it should surprise no one, that our liberties are undermined, the economy becomes overextended, and our involvement worldwide becomes prohibitive.

Liberty Should Not Be Sacrificed in Times of War

Out of fear of being labeled unpatriotic, most citizens become compliant and accept the argument that some loss of liberty is required to fight the war in order to remain safe. This is a bad trade-off in my estimation, especially when done in the name of patriotism.

Loyalty to the state and to autocratic leaders is substituted for true patriotism—that is, a willingness to challenge the state and defend the country, the people, and the culture. The more difficult the times, the stronger the admonition becomes that the leaders be not criticized.

Because the crisis atmosphere of war supports the growth of the state, any problem invites an answer by declaring "war"—even on social and economic issues. This elicits patriotism in support of various government solutions while enhancing the power of the state. Faith in government coercion and a lack of understanding of how free societies operate, encourages big government liberals and big government conservatives to manufacture a war psychology to demand political

Senator Russell Feingold Offers a Dissenting View of the President's War Policy

I cannot support an Iraq policy that makes our enemies stronger and our own country weaker, and that is why I will not support staying the course the President has set. If Iraq were truly the solution to our national security challenges, this gamble with the future of the military and with our own economy might make sense. If Iraq, rather than such strategically more significant countries as Saudi Arabia and Pakistan, were really at the heart of the global fight against violent Islamist terrorism, this might make some sense. If it were true that fighting insurgents in Baghdad meant that we would not have to fight them elsewhere, all of the costs of this policy might make some sense. But these things are not true. Iraq is not the silver bullet in the fight against global terrorist networks. . . . Meanwhile the costs of staying this course indefinitely, the consequences of weakening America's military and America's economy, loom more ominously before us with each passing week. There is no leadership in simply hoping for the best.

Russell Feingold,
"How the President's Policy Is Weakening America,"
Statement delivered to the U.S. Senate, September 29, 2005.

loyalty for domestic policy just as is required in foreign affairs. The long-term cost in dollars spent and liberties lost is neglected as immediate needs are emphasized.

It is for this reason that we have multiple perpetual wars going on simultaneously. Thus the war on drugs, against gun ownership, poverty, illiteracy, and terrorism, as well as our foreign military entanglements, are endless.

All this effort promotes the growth of statism at the expense of liberty. A government designed for a free society should do the opposite: prevent the growth of statism and preserve liberty. Once a war of any sort is declared, the message is sent out not to object or you will be declared unpatriotic. Yet, we must not forget that the true patriot is the one who protests in spite of the consequences, condemnation or ostracism, or even imprisonment that may result.

Rejecting Involuntary Servitude

Non-violent protesters of the tax code are frequently imprisoned—whether they are protesting the code's unconstitutionality or the war that the tax revenues are funding.

Resisters to the military draft, or even to selective service registration, are threatened and imprisoned for challenging this threat to liberty.

Statism depends on the idea that the government owns us and citizens must obey. Confiscating the fruits of our labor through the income tax is crucial to the health of the state. The draft, or even the mere existence of the selective service, emphasizes that we will march off to war at the state's pleasure. A free society rejects all notions of involuntary servitude whether by draft or the confiscation of the fruits of our labor through the personal income tax.

A more sophisticated and less well known technique for enhancing the state is the manipulation and transfer of wealth through the flat monetary system operated by the secretive Federal Reserve. Protestors against this unconstitutional system of paper money are considered unpatriotic criminals and at times are imprisoned for their beliefs. The fact that, according to the Constitution, only gold and silver are legal tender and paper money is outlawed, matters little. The principle of patriotism is turned on its head.

Whether it's with regard to the defense of welfare spending at home, confiscatory income tax, an immoral monetary system, or support for a war fought under false pretense without a legal declaration, the defenders of liberty and the Constitution are portrayed as unpatriotic while those who support these programs are seen as the patriots. If there's a "war" going on, supporting the state's efforts to win the war is expected at all costs. No dissent!

The real problem is that those who love the state too often advocate policies that lead to military action. At home they are quite willing to produce a crisis atmosphere and claim a war is needed to solve the problem. Under these conditions the people are more willing to bear the burden of paying for the war, and to carelessly sacrifice liberties which they are told is necessary.

The ... years [between 2001 and 2007] have been quite beneficial to the "health of the state," which comes at the expense of personal liberty. Every enhanced unconstitutional power of the state can only be achieved at the expense of individual liberty.

Periodical Bibliography

The following articles have been selected to supplement the diverse views presented in this chapter.

James A. Bryant Jr.   "Using History to Save Our Nation," *Education Digest*, November 2005.

Kathryn Cantrell   "Un-Volunteering," *Peace Review*, January-March 2007.

Nancy Gibbs   "What We've Learned," *Time*, September 11, 2006.

David P. Gushee   "What's Right About Patriotism," *Christianity Today*, July 2006.

Clyde Haberman   "Some Give All; Others Go Shopping," *New York Times*, November 24, 2006.

Lawrence F. Kaplan   "American Idle," *New Republic*, September 12, 2005.

Joe Klein   "The Danger of Yellow Ribbon Patriotism," *Time*, August 29, 2005.

George McGovern   "Patriotism Is Nonpartisan," *Nation*, April 11, 2005.

James Schlesinger   "Patriotism in Our Era," *Vital Speeches of the Day*, April 2007.

Roger Scruton   "The Culture of Repudiation," *American Spectator*, March 2007.

Donald W. Shriver   "Honest Patriotism," *America*, July 2, 2007.

Garth Stewart   "Stay and Fight," *Washington Monthly*, June 2007.

David Weigel   "When Patriots Dissent," *Reason*, November 2005.

Jeffrey Zaslow   "Patriotism, Then and Now," *Wall Street Journal*, July 1, 2005.

CHAPTER 4

Can American Values Bridge Cultural Divides?

Chapter Preface

Many American policy analysts who support a sustained U.S. presence in Iraq acknowledge that victory over resistance forces in that nation will not be achieved through military means alone. In the second year of Iraq's occupation, Joseph Ghougassian, a U.S. ambassador and a member of the now-defunct Coalition Provisional Authority in Iraq, explained that utilizing the mass media in Iraq was a necessary—if overlooked—method of winning the hearts and minds of the Iraqi people and convincing neighboring Muslim nations of America's altruistic intentions. Ghougassian stated, "To counter the negative image many Arabs have about the U.S. forces fighting in Iraq, Al–Hurra TV [an American satellite channel broadcasting in Arabic to the Middle East] should develop programs that invite Arab American military personnel to speak about their experience in the U.S. Armed Forces and their fighting of the terrorists in Iraq. Al–Hurra should also invite Iraqis to speak about the changes they are experiencing in their new life of freedom since the downfall of [Iraqi president] Saddam [Hussein]."

Beyond television, Ghougassian suggested opening other routes to cultural exchange that would facilitate communication in the region and undermine the negative images of American imperialism broadcast in the region. He advocated the creation of Internet discussion sites and the foundation of "American-style" universities to educate Arabs "on such topics as democracy, human rights, freedom from political coercion, free elections, new constitution guaranteeing a bill of individual rights, and other matters of concern." Such means of conveying American ideals to the Arab world are, to Ghougassian and others, the soft power counterpart to the hard power policies that brought the U.S. military to Iraq. Soft power, then, does not involve the coercion of others but instead subtly entices them to want the values America is selling.

Whether America can influence the Iraqi people and the greater Arab community with soft power initiatives is unknown. Former Secretary of Defense Donald Rumsfeld, for one, discounted soft power as too vague and transitory to determine U.S. foreign policy. His successor, Robert Gates, however, told an assembly of U.S. military officers in 2007 that "the most important military component in the war on terror is not the fighting we do ourselves, but how well we enable and empower our partners to defend and govern themselves." He supports the use of American civilians to mentor the Iraqi people in everything from rebuilding schools to verifying election results. As for the outcome of this soft power diplomacy, Gates added, "Success will be less a matter of imposing one's will and more a function of shaping behavior—of friends, adversaries and, most importantly, the people in-between."

In the following chapter, political and cultural analysts debate whether America can easily sell its values to the Middle East and other parts of the globe. Some insist the influence of America's soft power has already declined, leaving much of the world antagonistic to U.S. cultural exports. Others insist that only by fostering democracy, human rights, and other American values that have a universal appeal will the United States effectively bridge the cultural divides that have often hampered U.S. diplomacy and foreign policy agendas.

> *"We ... know, as Muslims and Christians, that recognizing our common humanity is both necessary and possible, and we know further that this recognition of the universality of core human values is a part of our religious understanding and a part of our religious duty."*

Christianity and Islam Share Important Values

David Blankenhorn

David Blankenhorn is founder and president of the Institute for American Values, a private, nonpartisan organization devoted to research and public education on issues of family and civil society. In the following viewpoint, Blankenhorn addresses Muslim scholars in Oman in hopes of fostering friendship based on shared values between Christianity and Islam. Blankenhorn suggests that both religions see divinity in all humanity and share a love of freedom of conscience and worship. He hopes these common values can inspire Muslims and Christians to work together to bridge the cultural divide.

David Blankenhorn, "The Clash of Civilizations or Global Civil Society?" Presented at the Grand Mosque, Muscat, Oman, March 14, 2005, Institute for American Values (americanvalues.org). Reproduced by permission.

As you read, consider the following questions:

1. What was the name of the letter to the world that sixty scholars wrote in response to the attacks of September 11, 2001?

2. As Blankenhorn explains, what three questions did the sixty U.S. scholars ask in their open letter to the world?

3. According to Blankenhorn, what two suggestions did he and his fellow thinkers make to American leaders in seeking a productive dialogue with the Arab world?

As-Salamu Alaykum. I am deeply grateful for the opportunity to visit your beautiful country, and I am honored to be with you today in this distinguished hall of learning, and in this great center of religious faith and devotion. . . .

We are two very different societies, of course, each with its own distinctive traditions and gifts, but we also have much in common. I am a Christian. One of my favorite verses from our Holy Bible says: "Do we not all have one Father? Has not one God created us?" And I have read in your Holy Koran this beautiful verse (49:13): "O mankind! We have created you from a male and female, and made you into nations and tribes, that you may know one another. Verily, the most honorable of you with Allah is the one who is more pious. Verily, Allah is all knowing, all aware." These and similar verses from our holy scriptures remind us not only of the great historical similarities between Christianity and Islam, with their common roots in the faith of Abraham and Isaac, and not only of the high degree of religiosity in both of our societies, but also that both of our great faith traditions, Islam and Christianity, tend to be universalistic in their outlook.

Universal Values

When we are truest to our faith—when we are pious—both Muslims and Christians seek to understand and relate sympathetically to humanity as a whole. We both are willing to recognize and even emphasize the many ways in which the particular values of our religions are linked to, and contribute to, the universal values of humankind. Because we know that we all have one Father, we can, when we are pious, try to see the spark of the divine—see the essential, God-given dignity—in every human person. Because we know that Allah made us different so that we may know and understand one another, we can, when we are pious, try our best to exclude no human being, and no society anywhere, from the circle of our kinship and from the requirement of equal moral regard.

This is our shared calling. This is our shared vision. Too often, of course, we fail in that calling. Too often we are blind and arrogant and narrow. Too often we are not pious. Certainly that is true of Christians. Critics of religion, in both the West and the East, often make this charge, and the first thing we must confess, I think, with great sadness, is that too often the charge is accurate.

But there is also a basis of hope and confidence for people of the book who would also be citizens of the world. For we also know, as Muslims and Christians, that recognizing our common humanity is both necessary and possible, and we know further that this recognition of the universality of core human values is a part of our religious understanding and a part of our religious duty. That is important. That is a strong, vital foundation on which we can stand, and work together, seeking to contribute as we can, and as we must, to building a world community based on justice, tolerance, and human dignity. . . .

Seeking Answers to Important Questions

Soon after the attacks [of September 11, 2001], I began exchanging ideas and reactions with some leading American scholars and public intellectuals who are affiliated with the Institute for American Values, the private, nonpartisan "think tank" which I direct and helped to found in 1987, and which has focused most of its work on public policies and cultural values regarding marriage, the family, child well-being, and civil society. Soon after September 11, we knew that we must broaden and deepen our focus in order first to understand, and then also perhaps to influence, the new situation before us.

On February 12, 2002—six months after 9/11 and on the birthday of Abraham Lincoln, perhaps our most revered president—sixty of us released to the world a public letter. We called the document, *What We're Fighting For: A Letter from America*. The co-authors and signatories included Jean Bethke Elshtain of the University of Chicago, Francis Fukuyama of Johns Hopkins University, William Galston of the University of Maryland and a former policy advisor to President Clinton, Mary Ann Glendon of Harvard Law School, Robert George of Princeton University, Samuel Huntington of Harvard, James Turner Johnson of Rutgers, former U.S. Senator Daniel Patrick Moynihan, Michael Walzer of the Institute for Advanced Studies in Princeton, James Q. Wilson, formerly of Harvard and UCLA, and numerous other prominent voices from across the human sciences and across the political spectrum.

Basically, the letter seeks to understand the meaning of the attacks of September 11, both for the United States and the world, and to defend on moral grounds the use of U.S. military force against the perpetrators and supporters of these attacks. This letter from America to the world asks, and seeks to answer, three main questions.

The first question is: "What are American values?" We asked the question because we believe that we were attacked not only, and perhaps not even primarily, because of the policies of our government, but also because of the qualities of our civil society and our overall way of life. So what is that way of life? What do we Americans value? We list some of the values of which we are not proud: our frequently excessive consumerism, our individualism that can lead to self-centeredness and the weakening of the family, and our frequently vulgar entertainment industry.

But we also list other values that we view as much more positive. The idea that all persons are created equal. The idea that moral truths exist and are accessible to all people. The idea that our understanding of the truth is always imperfect, so that most disagreements about values call for civility, openness to other views, and reasonable argument in pursuit of truth. And finally, the importance of freedom of conscience and freedom of religion. We say in the letter—and we now realize that we should have made this point much more clearly—that the best and most important of these values do not belong only to America, but are also the shared inheritance of all people of goodwill everywhere. We believe that these values are worth fighting for.

Looking for Moral Justification

The second question is: "What about God?" In trying to understand the meaning of 9/11, is religion a part of the solution or a part of the problem? We answer this question—and most of the signatories to the letter are persons of religious faith and commitment—by arguing for the importance of religious freedom as a fundamental right of all people in every nation.

The final question concerns the morality of the use of force. In response to the attacks of September 11, is the use of violence morally justified? To answer this question, we draw upon what we call just war theory—a broad and well-developed body of religious and ethical teachings about the use of force that dates back many centuries, and that has important roots in Islam, Christianity, and other diverse religions, and well as (more recently) in secular moral traditions. The great value of just war theory—its great contribution to the possibility of justice in the world—is its insistence that we think about war in universal categories and apply universal

American Muslims Should Prove Their Love of Liberty and Tolerance

American Muslims . . . should preach and promote the universal human values of free speech, inquiry, and exchange; individual liberty; toleration; and representative government. And they should use their cultural institutions to raise a new generation of Muslims who will incorporate these principles into their hearts and minds, in the same way that millions of other immigrants—Catholics from Italy and Ireland, Jews from Eastern Europe and Russia, Buddhists from Asia, Hindus and Sikhs from India—have done and continue to do. Tolerance does not mean agreement with other religions or lifestyles. It does mean a deep commitment to respecting the rights and freedom of those with whom you might disagree.

Edward Hudgins, "Allah Bless America,"
Navigator, *November-December 2002.*

moral rules to the conduct of war. For if we think about war in this way—if we seek to apply universal principles of justice to the use of force—we quickly see that most wars throughout history were not morally justified. Indeed, throughout its history, the primary function of just war theory has been to limit the use of force, not to justify or authorize it.

At the same time, there are times when the use of force is necessary, primarily in order to protect the innocent from certain harm. We argue in our letter that the attacks of September 11 constitute one of those times when the use of force as a response to calamitous acts of violence and injustice is not only morally permitted, but morally required. Our letter states: "Organized killers with global reach now threaten all of us. In the name of universal human morality, and fully conscious of the restrictions and requirements of a just war, we support our government's, and our society's, decision to use force of arms against them."

Strong Reaction from Muslim World

We concluded our letter with these words: "We wish especially to reach out to our brothers and sisters in Muslim societies. We say to you forthrightly: We are not enemies, but friends. We must not be enemies. We have so much in common. There is so much that we must do together. Your human dignity, no less than ours—your rights and opportunities for a good life, no less than ours—are what we believe we're fighting for. We know that, for some of you, mistrust of us is high, and we know that we Americans are partly responsible for that mistrust. But we must not be enemies. In hope, we wish to join with you and all people of goodwill to build a just and lasting peace."

Coming as it did at the time of the U.S. military intervention in Afghanistan to replace the Taliban regime, which had openly supported and collaborated with al Qaeda, the release of our letter drew an immediate and intense reaction, particularly in Europe and in the Arab and Muslim world. Most of the reaction was strongly negative. For example, 153 scholars and public intellectuals in Saudi Arabia issued a detailed and highly critical reply to our letter. (Interestingly, our reply to them, which was published in *al-Hayat*, led to that issue of *al-Hayat* being banned from Saudi Arabia by the Saudi government.) In fact, we spent much of the rest of 2002, in particular, in intensive public debates and written exchanges with groups and individuals from around the world who had responded to our public letter. It was a remarkable experience. I, for one, had never experienced anything quite like it. . . .

Face-to-Face Exchange

But here the story takes a turn. In 2003, I met with Hassan Mneimneh, a Lebanese-American author and leader, and Professor Ridwan El-Sayyed, a distinguished scholar in Islamic studies from the Lebanese University in Beirut. Professor Ridwan is here with me on the podium today and is kindly translating my comments into Arabic for you. He had organized a special issue of a scholarly journal containing analyses of and replies to *What We're Fighting For*. In that meeting in 2003, an idea was born. Instead of more written exchanges, how about face-to-face meetings? Instead of debate, how about dialogue? How about bringing together leading Arab and Muslim public intellectuals, along with their U.S. counterparts, for careful, sustained discussions of these critical issues? For in a time of war and discussions of war, and in a world facing the grim prospect of religious and even civilizational polarization, which tasks facing intellectuals from East and West are more important than finding a time and place to reason together, in the hope of finding common ground on the meaning of civil society and the basic conditions for human flourishing? ...

I hope and pray that our meeting today can in some way contribute to realizing this goal, and for that opportunity I am deeply grateful to you.

America Must Build Trust in the Arab World

Let me conclude my comments by seeking to generalize a bit from the story that I have just told you. Drawing on our experience with the "Letter from America" and with our Malta Forum [i.e., the first arranged face-to-face meeting in 2004] let me respectfully offer several suggestions to U.S. civic and political leaders, and several to Arab and Muslim civic and political leaders, who seek to participate in serious dialogue and help to make real progress toward the global civil society.

Here are two suggestions for U.S. leaders to consider.

First, despite the example that I am setting here today, lecture less and listen more. We Americans often tend to think that we know other people's situation better than they do; that our values are, or should be, their values; and that other people could solve their problems in short order if only they would follow American advice. Let me speak with understatement: Often this is not true.

Relatedly, we Americans often seem to think that our views and positions, both governmental and nongovernmental, can be effectively communicated to Arab and Muslim publics primarily in the form of top-down, sanitized propaganda dispensed through non-interactive means. Again, with understatement: Often this is not true. U.S. ideas, positions, and values can be much more effectively communicated to Arab and Muslim publics as part of a naturally pluralistic reality, primarily in the form of peer-to-peer, face-to-face discussions involving U.S. opinion leaders and willing and capable Arab and Muslim interlocutors. If U.S. leaders can move in this direction, they may do much to build trust and to correct the distorted images, widespread today among Arab and Muslim public intellectuals, of a U.S. superpower bent on the exploitation and subjugation of the Arab and Muslim world.

Second, be more consistent when it comes to advocating democracy and human rights. The mistrust of American intentions, which is strong in much of the Arab and Muslim world today, is partly due to the fact that, for decades, America has compromised its commitment to democracy and human rights by frequently supporting unaccountable rulers who mistreat their people. In his recent Inaugural Address, President [George W.] Bush alluded to this legacy, particularly in the Middle East, and vowed to correct it. From now on, the President said, democracy and human rights are centerpieces of U.S. foreign policy—not just sometimes, but always; and not just in some places, but everywhere. May it be so.

Muslim Nations Must Temper Their Suspicion of America

Now here are two suggestions for Arab and Muslim leaders to consider.

First, do not underestimate America's influence in your societies, but do not overestimate it either. There is a tendency among some Arab and Muslim commentators to blame America for nearly all of their problems, even including some obviously homegrown problems, and similarly to imagine that whatever needs to be changed can he accomplished by a change in U.S. policy. Often this is not true. American actions and intentions do matter, of course, but obviously not nearly as much as the actions and intentions of Arabs and Muslims themselves.

Relatedly, do not assume that American leaders are always operating in good faith, but please do not assume bad faith either. Instead, trust, but verify. For example, President Bush just committed the United States to pushing hard and consistently for progress in human rights and democracy in the Middle East and the world. Surely, even for those who may usually be skeptical, this is good news, or at least potentially good news. Perhaps this is a basis from which people of goodwill on both sides can work to reduce mistrust and seek out ways to work together for positive social change.

Second, seek out ways to build on, and contribute to, the democracy and civil society movements that are already growing in the Arab and Muslim world. These movements are potentially extremely important, both for you and for the world. They are reasons for great hope. They are the chimes of freedom. Today you may be—we all may be—in a moment of great opportunity. Please seize it. Others can wish you well, and perhaps help a bit, or at least get out of your way, but of course in the final analysis only you can do the main work of building and expanding democratic freedoms and human rights in your societies. If you seize this moment, great progress is possible, and others from around the world will learn from you and follow you.

Our vision is a bold one. What do we seek? Working together, we seek to replace the clash of civilizations with a global civil society guided by universal human values and based on the principles of justice and tolerance. I believe that this is the great calling of our generation, a true task for those who would be pious, and I look forward to working with you in the months and years ahead to make this great change in our world.

> "While [Christianity and Islam] may share many historical persons and events in common, there is still an unbridgeable gap between them."

Christianity and Islam Do Not Share Values

Dean Robinson

In the following viewpoint, Dean Robinson, a writer for the Baptist Pillar, *a news organ of the Baptist Church in Canada, insists that Islam and Christianity are incompatible. In Robinson's view, Islam is a false religion that demands blind adherence from its followers and calls them to take up arms to slay all nonbelievers. He claims that those Christians who try to "dialogue" with Muslims are misguided because Islam has proven itself an intolerant worldview that rejects the core beliefs of Christianity.*

As you read, consider the following questions:

1. What evidence does Robinson reveal to prove his claim that Islam is an intolerant religion?

2. What two quotes from the Koran does Robinson utilize to suggest that "compromise, concession, or agreement between true Christianity and orthodox Islam" cannot exist?

Dean Robinson, "False Religion of Islam," *Baptist Pillar*, Reproduced by permission.

3. Instead of dialoguing with Muslims, what does the author suggest is the Christian duty toward Muslims?

Islam is not a religious cult in the strictest sense of the word but it is a major world religion, a false religion vastly different and opposed to Christianity. Islam is the fastest growing religion in the world with one out of every five people on the face of the earth being a Muslim. It is considered to be one of the four largest religions in the world, behind Christianity, Judaism, and Hinduism. It is estimated that by the year 2010, Islam will move ahead of Judaism to become the second largest religion in America. Hundreds of millions of people all over the world have embraced the Islamic faith to where entire countries are ruled and dominated by Islamic teachings, practices, and laws. Islam is a religious, social, and political force which every born-again Christian and every American should be aware of. . . .

Islam Offers the World Submission or Death

It is traditionally taught that there is no ceremony, no ritual involved in a person who wants to become a Muslim. All one has to do is to believe and say: "There is no god but Allah and Muhammed is his prophet." After saying this, the person is obligated to do all the duties of Islam. One must remember that the word "Muslim" means: *one who submits*. Islam basically offers the world two choices: the Koran (conversion) or the sword (death). According to the teaching of the Koran, conversion to Islam can either be by persuasion or force. We must understand that the spread of Islam through the centuries has been carried out largely on the battlefield. Islam has been advanced by the widespread use of war, torture, and force of arms. Islam has swept over the world slaughtering Jews and Christians alike. Islam is a fighting religion. Conquest is a religious duty in Islam. The Koran urges Muslims to take up arms against the "infidel" (anyone who is not a Muslim). The Koran specifically says: "When ye encounter unbelievers, strike off their heads until ye have made a great slaughter among them, and bind them in bonds." In another place it says: "those who fight against you, kill them wherever ye shall find them . . . You Allah are our protector. Give us victory therefore over the infidel nations." "Kill thine enemy" is the practical teaching of Islam.

The Koran is the final authority in Islam. It is the recordings of all the visions and revelations that Muhammed supposedly received directly from Allah. There were 114 in total. These revelations in the Koran are believed by Muslims to have come to Muhammed over a period of twenty-three years. The Koran is divided into 114 "suras" or chapters and contains many quotations and references to the Bible. Quoting from one source: "The Koran offers a religion that relies upon methods of violence and force—a doctrine of holy wars that brings inducements to political revolution and assassinations which have produced wars and tragedies unimaginable. The Koran offers a theology that is distinctly anti-Christ, claiming a method of salvation based entirely upon works."

Islam claims to revere the writings of all the supposed great prophets of the world yet the Muslims definitely exalt and honor the "prophecy" of Muhammed (i.e. the Koran) above the Scriptures and any other religious writings. Muslims believe that Muhammed is the prophet who fully revealed the final truth and they will not compromise that belief. A leaflet prepared by the *Institute of Islamic Information and Education* states: "Muhammed is the very last Prophet of God to mankind. He is the final Messenger of God. His message was and is still to the Christians, the Jews, and the rest of mankind. He was sent to those religious people to inform them about the true mission of Jesus, Moses, David, Jacob, Isaac, and Abraham." The leaflet continues: "Muhammed is considered to be the summation and the culmination of all the prophets and messengers that came before him. He purified the previous messages from adulteration and completed the Message of

God for all humanity. He was entrusted with the power of explaining, interpreting, and living the teachings of the Koran." Muslims believe that all mankind must be brought into subjection to the teachings of the Koran in order to experience peace and blessing.

Rejecting Biblical Views

In the Koran, Islam is more than a religion; it is a complete way of life that includes political, economic, social as well as religious conduct. All Islam claims to follow the Koran but there are a multitude of interpretations and applications of it among Muslims.

At first glance to the general public, Islamic belief appears to be almost compatible with Christianity. Often people claim that the Muslims believe in the same God as Christians with the exception that they do not accept Jesus Christ. It is often said that Christians, Jews, and Muslims are worshipping the same God but in different ways. Muslims have capitalized on this misconception and now urge Christians and Jews to worship the one God (Allah) with them, and work together for solutions to the world's many social problems.

Based on the Koran, Muslims believe in one god (Allah but not the Trinity); they believe in God as the Creator and Jesus as a prophet (but not as Saviour); they believe in the resurrection of all (including animals), final judgment, and eternal punishment. They believe in all of these things but not according to the Bible's definition of these things. When you carefully study the Bible and compare it with the teachings of the Koran, it becomes obvious that the god of Islam is not the God of the Bible. Islam rejects the biblical doctrines of the Trinity and the Deity of Christ, among other things.

What Muslims Believe About God

For the Muslim, Allah is the only true God. The Muslim concept of Allah is not what God reveals Himself to be in the Bible. To say that God and Allah are two names for the same being reveals a lack of understanding of the Bible or the Koran or both. The Muslims teach there is no such thing as the "blasphemous" doctrine of the Trinity, i.e. the Godhead is One but exists in three Persons. Christians are referred to as unbelievers, infidels by the Muslims because they believe in the Trinity. In a booklet entitled *Christian Muslim Dialogue* on page 16, it states: "The Trinity is not biblical. The word 'trinity' is not even in the Bible or Bible dictionaries; it was never taught by Jesus and was never mentioned by him. There is no basis or proof in the Bible whatsoever for the acceptance of the Trinity." The Koran states that Christians worship three gods: God, Jesus, and Mary. It denies that there is a Trinity in the Godhead. It also says that those who say that God is a Trinity are to be severely punished: "Surely they are disbelievers those who said Allah is one of the three in a trinity. But there is none who has the right to be worshipped but one God (Allah). And if they cease not from what they say, verily a painful torment will befall the disbelievers among them."

The Muslim god is unapproachable by sinful man; he is so perfect and holy he can only communicate with mankind through a progression of angels and prophets. The Muslim god is a god of judgment, not grace; a god of wrath rather than love. Muslims have no concept of God as a loving and compassionate Father. Muslims never do refer to God as "Father;" they explain He would have to have a wife and children to be called such a name. This means, of course, that Muslims deny the deity of Christ. The Koran states: "It is not meet for Allah, the he should have any son. Allah forbid." Another quote plainly says: "God has no Son. . . ."

No Concession Between Islam and Christianity

For a true Muslim, the Koran is the "word of Allah," and is to be believed and practiced literally. Apart from being a Muslim, there is no hope for a person according to the Koran. The Ko-

Islam Is Incompatible with Democracy

Democracy means the rule of the *demos*, the common people, or what is now known as popular or national sovereignty.

In Islam, however, power belongs only to God: *al-hukm l'illah*. The man who exercises that power on earth is known as *Khalifat al-Allah*, the regent of God.

But even then the Khalifah or Caliph cannot act as legislator. The law has already been spelled out and fixed for ever by God.

The only task that remains is its discovery, interpretation and application.

That, of course, allows for a substantial space in which different styles of rule could develop.

But the bottom line is that no Islamic government can be democratic in the sense of allowing the common people equal shares in legislation.

Islam divides human activities into five categories from the permitted to the sinful, leaving little room for human interpretation, let alone ethical innovations.

What we must understand is that Islam has its own vision of the world and man's place in it.

To say that Islam is incompatible with democracy should not be seen as a disparagement of Islam.

On the contrary, many Muslims would see it as a compliment because they sincerely believe that their idea of rule by God is superior to that of rule by men which is democracy.

Amir Taheri, Remarks at debate
"Islam Is Incompatible with Democracy,"
May 19, 2004. www.benadorassociates.com.

ran says: "Whoso desires any other religion than Islam, that religion shall never be accepted from him, and in the next world he shall be among the lost." Another quote: "The true religion with God is Islam." These two quotes simply signify that there can be no compromise, concession, or agreement between true Christianity and orthodox Islam. . . .

Islam claims to be a religion of peace and tolerance when in fact it is characterized by violence and religious bigotry. It is the Christian's duty to diligently witness to, not dialogue with the Muslims. We must stand for the true Gospel and against all other false gospels. Islam has rejected the essential teachings of the Word of God. The so-called prophet Muhammed brought an erroneous message from a false spirit that is totally opposed to the Gospel of God's grace. The message of Islam is a curse, not a blessing. "There is only one true religion. It was prophesied in the Garden of Eden, typified in the days of Noah, confirmed to Abraham, Isaac, and Jacob, and realized in the Person and work of Jesus Christ."

There is no doubt that Muslims have a definite zeal for their god. They desire to follow Allah and express their worship of Allah through their lives. But the fact remains, Muslims need Christ and His saving Gospel which is still the power of God unto salvation to everyone that believeth. They need not only to hear and believe this life-changing Gospel of Jesus Christ, but they also need to see it demonstrated in the lives of believers to serve as an example of what the Lord can do with a life that is totally and truly surrendered and submitted unto Him. Islam offers this world two choices: the Koran (conversion) or the sword (death). Bible-believing Christians have only one choice to offer the world: the Cross and empty tomb of Jesus Christ.

In this age of ecumenicalism and tolerance, many people would like to emphasize the resemblances and similarities between Islam and Christianity. While the two religions may share many historical persons and events in common, there is still an unbridgeable gap between them. "There is no possible compromise between biblical Christianity and Islam and none should be sought."

"The problems establishing democracy in societies historically unfamiliar with the concept are not insurmountable."

America Can Successfully Export Democracy

Richard Warren Field

Richard Warren Field asserts in the following viewpoint that America can spread democracy in the world. He maintains that for democracy to take hold, however, the people of undemocratic nations must desire democracy and receive assurances that their personal interests will be more secure under democracy than under their present ideology. Field states that these prerequisites— the belief in equality, the safeguarding of personal liberty, and the acknowledgement that prosperity can come through collective effort—are American values, but that all people seeking the benefits of democracy can easily adopt these values. Richard Warren Field is a musician, occasional columnist, and author of The Election, *a political novel.*

As you read, consider the following questions:

1. How does Field refute the notion that Islamic countries cannot embrace democracy?

2. How does Field use Maslow's Hierarchy of Needs in his argument about people's desire for freedom?

3. What element of Field's theory does he say was partly responsible for bringing down the Iron Curtain?

"Americans should not try to impose their way of life on other societies." "Some populations are not ready for democracy." "What is viable in one political culture may not be viable in another." These are some of the statements we hear from those who believe American foreign policy is too ambitious when the goal is to liberate societies captured by totalitarianism and replace those repressive governments with democracies. Those taking this position would argue that the supposed folly of "exporting democracy" has been demonstrated to Americans by the recent difficulties with establishing a functioning government in Iraq, and by the recent election of Hamas by Palestinians. They would also argue that American involvement in Vietnam in the 1960s and 1970s was the ultimate example of the proof of these statements.

Exporting Democracy Has Worked Previously

The problems establishing democracy in societies historically unfamiliar with the concept are not insurmountable, and any culture in the world is capable of maintaining a free, democratic system. We hear arguments that Islam is incompatible with democracy—that the Koran and Sharia/Islamic Law cannot coexist with a free society. But Turkey and Indonesia are functioning democracies with primarily Muslim populations. Each in its own way has reconciled Islamic tradition with a free, democratic society. Japan and Germany had little democratic tradition before their successful post World War II democracies were established. Both nations had been hijacked by fanatic extremists, and seemed completely unlikely candidates for democracy at the birth of their democracies. Many recently liberated Eastern European countries, with little tradition of democracy, have established thriving democracies. These democracy success stories span the globe, reflecting wide and varied religious, cultural and ethnic traditions.

So, why do some countries make an easier transition to democracy and freedom while others either have difficulties or fail? There are three worldviews, prevalent in American political culture, which need to be substantially present for a successful transition to occur. These could be called "American values," but they are not really culture-specific ideas. They are fundamental assumptions about the world, approaches to everyday life that are certainly American, but not exclusively American, and are transferable to all cultures. They are the equality ethic, the confidence of personal security, and a belief in mutual prosperity as opposed to a zero-sum game.

The People Must Believe That Democracy Is Possible

It is not enough for a society to pay lip service to the idea that all within its borders will be treated equally under the law. The people must believe such a world is possible. They must believe that equality of opportunity and social mobility will exist in their economic and political system as a fundamental, permanent element. Otherwise, members of the country will remain constantly fearful that one group can turn on another to dominate politically and economically, and elections will become power-plays between contending groups instead of processes where citizens make choices based on leadership and policies in the best interests of the entire nation. These contending groups could be Sunni and Shiite, Catholics and Protestant, or rich and poor. It is a problem not confined to Muslim societies alone, and it is a problem that can be addressed in Muslim societies trying to make the move from totalitarianism to democracy and freedom. The citizens of the country must develop a confidence that their society is fair. Though some in the society will always succumb to believing they are victims, the predominant sentiment across all the constituent groups of the society must be a confidence that all individuals are considered equal under the law.

The Confidence of Personal Security

We Americans like to emphasize the aspirations of human beings to live in freedom. The speeches of President [John F.] Kennedy of the 1960s, President [Ronald] Reagan of the 1980s and President George W. Bush of the 2000s are only recent examples of the expression of this American ideal. One of the most famous quotes from the American Revolution was Patrick Henry's unequivocal pronouncement: "Give me liberty or give me death." But in fact, this is not really the priority for a typical human being. When we look at Maslow's Hierarchy of Needs[1], we note that physical safety is the second most fundamental need, after the physical needs of food, water and air. "Freedom" comes well after physical safety. According to Maslow, it comes at least after the need for belonging. The need for freedom's placement in the Hierarchy of Needs arguably comes either under self-esteem, or self-actualization, both well after the priority of physical safety.

The point is that people are not going to be concerned about freedom if they are not fed, and not safe. Revolutions with a "give-me-liberty-or-give-me-death" rallying cry emerged either on the tide of rising expectations, like the American Revolution, or on the tide of desperation, where survival was at stake for the rebels. It is human nature to choose the certainty of survival in an unfree society over the uncertainty of survival in a society struggling to be free. People will long for the return of that repressive dictator and curse their liberators if their personal security seems to remain in unending jeopardy. So people must develop confidence that their personal

---

1. In 1943 psychologist Abraham Maslow created a chart reflecting human psychological growth that prioritizes the needs of most healthy individuals.

Only Democracy Can End Tyranny

Calling upon a free Middle East is not an impossible, Utopian dream. In fact, it is very effective and, ultimately, is the only effective method of ending tyranny. It is commonly known and accepted that Ronald Reagan's speeches in favor of freedom around the world inspired people to rise up against their tyrannical regimes. He was not afraid to say: our way is better and your way must change. This is exactly what we should be doing in the war on terrorism now.

Trying to fight tyranny solely militarily is ineffective and suicidal. We tried to fight communism militarily during Vietnam and lost. Even if we had won, it would not have mattered. When one tyrannical regime fell, another one would have just as soon taken its place. The same will happen with terrorism. Only when we attack terrorism at its root, by stating that tyranny and terrorism are morally repugnant and the world does not approve of regimes that torture their own and other people, will terrorism ultimately be eradicated.

We should not hesitate to advocate and enforce our enlightened way of life for the Iraqis or anywhere else.

Amber Pawlik,
"Exporting Freedom," MensNewsDaily,
May 9, 2004. www.mensnewsdaily.com.

security is assured or they will not accept a move to democracy as in their interests. An initial fight for liberation can be understood—an unending instability replacing the former regime will make the people long for the tyrant. This is because most people understand that if you give them death, liberty won't be much of an issue.

The Belief in Mutual Prosperity

Most importantly, and this may be the most American of these necessary worldviews, and the hardest to accept, is the belief that people can prosper together—they do not have to prosper at one another's expense. In classic game theory, it is the embrace of mutual gain over the zero-sum game. It is the idea that wealth is infinite, that prosperity creates prosperity, that we should want thriving neighbors because their prosperity benefits us. This may be the toughest, most progressive and truly modern concept of the three. It is counterintuitive—it was an incorrect view of the world until very recently. Throughout history, what one person had, another did not have. What one tribe had, another tribe did not have. In fact, what tribe one possessed might have been forcibly taken from tribe two. That concept evolved and extrapolated to ancient empires, and was inherited by the colonial powers of the nineteenth and twentieth centuries. It's the conservation of mass and energy principle applied to a concept of "conservation of wealth."

The zero-sum attitude, the idea that my neighbor's prosperity is probably at my expense, is ingrained in many societies. In fact, the more ancient societies, with the longer traditions of exploiters and exploited, struggling for finite shares of wealth and prosperity, arguably have the most difficult time accepting the mutual prosperity concept. Even the so-called first democracy of Ancient Greece built its democracy on the labor of a huge slave population.

But people from societies all over the world, from many different ethnic, religious and cultural traditions, have come to the United States, embraced mutual prosperity, and thrived. The American success story is the greatest argument against the zero-sum attitude. Doubters should be offered large doses of experience with the American version of mutual prosperity. Most of us from the Iron Curtain era can offer at least a few stories of visitors from the Soviet Union or Eastern Europe who were overwhelmed with the vast and varied offerings of consumer goods as contrasted with the lines and shortages in their own countries. I recall one woman visitor who actually believed the American supermarket she visited was staged for her benefit—such a store could not really exist in the world. (Her government told her to expect such propaganda stunts by the imperialist Americans.) The knowledge of such possibilities certainly helped the Free World's assault on the Iron Curtain, and the quick acceptance of democracy and embrace of Americans by many of the newly liberated Eastern European nations.

Toward Global Democracy

Identifying these three elements helps us define the transition problem for the nations trying to emerge from totalitarianism to democracy, and pulls the issue out of culture and religion specific biases, where it does not belong. The way these elements should be addressed will vary from situation to situation. And addressing them will be easier in some circumstances than in others. But by understanding these fundamentally necessary worldviews for a thriving democracy—and by realizing that while they have a strong American character, they are not exclusively American, they did not originate solely in America, and they have a universal appeal that transcends America—we can try to continue the spread of democracy and freedom at every opportunity, maybe one day to every corner of the world. Let freedom and democratically functioning governments rule the world, evolving in their own unique ways. Then we can all embrace a mutual prosperity for humanity. And we can consider that if there will ever be a world government, these three worldviews will be on hand, permeating the international political culture. If that day comes, we will be able to talk about mutually assured prosperity, replacing the scary Cold War concept of "mutually assured destruction."

> *"The tendency to conflate America, and American international interests, with righteousness can too easily lead to demonization of rival nations."*

America Faces Serious Obstacles in Exporting Democracy

Anatol Lieven and John Hulsman

Anatol Lieven is a senior researcher at the New America Foundation, a nonprofit public policy organization. John Hulsman is a contributing editor at the National Interest, *a foreign policy periodical. In the following viewpoint, Lieven and Hulsman argue that America's attempts to export democracy will not guarantee a peaceful world. In their view, efforts to export democracy have often been perceived as another form of American imperialism, imposing Western ideals upon nations that do not share Western views. Furthermore, the authors claim that exporting democracy has often been undertaken to weaken unfriendly governments instead of with the intent of bringing freedom to the oppressed. Lieven and Hulsman state that although bringing democracy to other parts of the world can be a worthwhile goal,*

Anatol Lieven and John Hulsman, "The Folly of Exporting Democracy," September 12, 2006. www.tompaine.com. Reproduced by permission of the authors.

the pursuit of this aim will become meaningless—even danger-
ous—if nondemocratic nations embrace democracy in name and
not in principle.

As you read, consider the following questions:

1. According to the authors, why is the democracy movement in Eastern Europe a poor model on which to plan
   the democratization of the Middle East?
2. What two elements do the authors believe must be
   present in each democracy to maintain a general commitment to coexist peacefully with other democracies?
3. What are Franklin Delano Roosevelt's "Four Freedoms"
   and why do Lieven and Hulsman contend that these
   freedoms do not necessarily guarantee democracy?

A certain awareness of the limits on American power is
growing among the wiser U.S. policy elites as a result of
the disasters into which the [George W.] Bush administration
has led the United States. Even in these circles, however, a very
widespread belief exists that in the former Soviet Union and
in the Muslim world, America can compensate for these weak-
nesses by encouraging the spread of democracy. The idea that
"democracy" will solve all problems is also used as a conscious
or unconscious excuse to avoid having to think seriously about
negotiating compromise solutions to a range of disputes in
the Middle East, and especially, of course, the Israeli-
Palestinian conflict—since this would require a willingness to
show moral courage in facing the inevitable backlash within
the United States.

This faith and attitude is shared not just by neoconservatives and liberal hawks, but by a majority of the leaderships of
both parties, by majorities in establishment think tanks like
the Carnegie Endowment and the Brookings Institution and
by much of the foreign policy bureaucracy. It is also not a

fantasy cooked up by the neo-conservatives, but has deep roots in certain strands of the American tradition. It is also often tragically mistaken.

What Worked in Eastern Europe May Not Work Elsewhere

The element of classical tragedy is that spreading democracy is a noble and worthwhile goal. A world in which democracies are more widespread, more secure, and more firmly anchored should indeed be part of the American legacy to humanity. The errors lie in believing that the spread of democracy consists of progress down a single known path to a fixed and pre-ordained goal: that this progress can and should be linked to the achievement of short- and medium-term American foreign policy goals; that true democrats in other countries should be expected to invariably support those goals, even if they conflict with the national interests of their own countries; and that democracy can substitute for wise diplomacy.

Insofar as this analysis is based on anything other than ideological faith, it draws almost exclusively on the history of Eastern Europe during and after the fall of communism. But as [American philosopher and political economist] Francis Fukuyama and others now have argued that the East European case is unique and must not be universalized. In Eastern Europe, nationalism was mobilized behind political and economic reform in a way that cannot be replicated elsewhere—least of all in the Middle East, where much of Arab and Iranian nationalism is bitterly anti-American.

East Europeans committed themselves to democracy and reform as a way of escaping the hated influence of Moscow and fulfilling what they regard as their historically mandated national destinies of joining the West. In Eastern Europe, therefore, nationalism, a pro-American outlook and support for democracy all went together. Moreover, the push of nationalism in Eastern Europe was added to the tremendous pull of NATO and European Union [E.U.] membership, and the assistance of European Union aid. But E.U. membership is assuredly not being offered to Egypt, Saudi Arabia or Iran.

Democracy Must Be Linked to National Interest

In the Muslim world, both spreading democracy and attracting support for U.S. policies will be possible only if enough Muslims think that this is not only in their personal interest, but also in their patriotic interest. Preaching democracy and freedom at them is useless if they associate the adoption of Western-style democracy with national humiliation and the sacrifice of vital national interests.

The problem is that this democratist thinking is borne of an American culture that makes it very difficult for many Americans to understand other peoples' nationalisms. The tendency to conflate America, and American international interests, with righteousness can too easily lead to demonization of rival nations. This is especially true where these nations are ruled by non-democratic systems that Americans instinctively see as illegitimate. Many of the subjects of those states may share this feeling. On the other hand, on foreign and security issues, those states may well enjoy the support of the great majority of their peoples—at least when it comes to a defense of national interests and an angry rejection of foreign pressure. So dismissing the views of other states because those states are not democratic can therefore easily become a dismissal of the views of their peoples too, even when these views are expressed by such Westernized and liberal figures as the journalists of Al Jazeera and Al Arabiya.

Democracy as a Tool of Foreign Policy Aims

Among neoconservatives and liberal hawks, the desire to spread democracy can also take a form explicitly dedicated to the weakening or even destruction of other states, even ones that are by no means fully-fledged enemies of the United States. This kind of thinking has been given a tremendous impetus by the way in which mass "democratic" movements (which were, in fact, mostly nationalist) helped destroy the Soviet Union. Thus in a piece urging a tough U.S. strategy of confronting and weakening China, Max Boot of *The Wall Street Journal* wrote:

> Beyond containment, deterrence, and economic integration lies a strategy that the British never employed against either Germany or Japan—internal subversion. Sorry, the polite euphemisms are "democracy promotion" and "human rights protection," but these amount to the same thing: The freer China becomes, the less power the Communist oligarchy will enjoy. The United States should aim to "Taiwanize" the mainland—to spread democracy through such steps as increased radio broadcasts and Internet postings ... In general, the U.S. government should elevate the issue of human rights in our dealings with China. We need to champion Chinese dissidents, intellectuals, and political prisoners, and help make them as famous as [Eastern European dissidents] Andrei Sakharov, Václav Havel, and Lech Walesa.

Is it surprising that faced with these perspectives, not just the Communist regime but many ordinary Chinese and Russians view the U.S. preaching of democracy as part of a plan to weaken or even destroy their countries, irrespective of the cost to their populations?

Peace Has Prerequisites

In terms of U.S. national interests, the argument for the spreading of democracy in the world is based on the idea of the "Democratic Peace": the belief, repeatedly stated by President Bush and other officials, that "democracies don't fight other democracies." It is indeed true that established democracies don't fight each other, but only if other very important factors are either added to the equation or removed from it—

www.caglecartoons.com/espanol

© 2004 Simanca Osmani, and PoliticalCartoons.com.

which means this is not true as far as much of the world is concerned and for the foreseeable future.

Two elements must be present. First, there must be the legal and civil institutions that we in the West think of as naturally accompanying democracy, but are, in fact, absent from most quasi-democracies around the world. Second, a nation must have prosperity, which creates middle classes with a real commitment to democracy and spreads well-being through enough of the population that the masses accept being led by the middle classes rather than some variety of populist demagogue, as is increasingly the case in Latin America today.

The first element that has to be taken out of the mix—and cannot be—is nationalism, or some mixture of mutually hostile ethno-religious allegiances, as in Iraq. As Edward Mansfield and Jack Snyder have convincingly argued in their book

Electing to Fight that new and weak democracies are, if anything, more likely to fight each other than established autocra-
cies, as new freedom allows the public expression of long-
suppressed national grievances, which are then exploited by
opportunist politicians. The fall of communism led to a whole
row of such cases in the Balkans and the Caucasus: The governments and movements which fought each other there in
the 1990s were elected and mostly genuinely popular.

In the Middle East, we have already seen electoral victory
for radical Islamist forces in Iran, the Shia areas of Lebanon,
the Palestinian territories and the Pashtun areas of Pakistan.
To judge by recent limited elections in Saudi Arabia and Egypt,
radicals would also win free votes there if the authorities permitted it.

In the long run, democracy is indeed necessary for progress
and stability in the greater Middle East and for the defeat of
terrorism and extremism. But moderate, nonaggressive, reasonably pro-Western democracies can only be established in
the long run if the social, cultural and institutional foundations for them are laid by successful economic development—
and this is a generational process. Furthermore, there is no
chance of Arab democratic feeling developing in a moderate
and pro-Western direction unless the U.S. changes many of its
existing policies in the Middle East and shows a respect—
democratic respect—for the opinions of ordinary people in
the region.

Democracy and Freedom
Are Not Synonymous

Even more strikingly, Washingtonian democratist orthodoxy
presents an understanding of freedom that is very distorted
from the one shared by most Americans and by the American
tradition. The founding document on which the moral philosophy of America's approach to the world over the past sixty
years is based is [Franklin Delano] Roosevelt's famous "Four

Freedoms" speech of 1941, setting out the great principles which inspired the Western allies during the Second World War. Those who haven't read them often assume that they must include the freedom to vote. Wrong. The four freedoms are freedom of speech and expression, freedom of worship, freedom from want and freedom from fear. Democracy as such is nowhere mentioned.

Of course, none of these freedoms can exist under a totalitarian state but they can all exist under a moderately authoritarian one—as they did in several states of Europe before 1914. Freedom from want and freedom from fear both require states that respect their citizens, but are also strong enough to protect them.

Also required are the rule of law, a reasonably independent and efficient judiciary and police, a law-abiding, honest and rational bureaucracy and a population that enjoys basic rights of labor, movement and free discussion. All of these rights can, and often have, existed in countries where the executive has been unelected. None exist in rotten contemporary "democracies" like the Philippines. All of these things require that the state be strong enough to protect its citizens from outside aggression, internal rebellion, uncontrolled crime, and oppression and exploitation by predatory elites, including the state's servants acting on their own account and for their own profit, like the police in so many countries. Francis Lieber, adviser to President [Abraham] Lincoln, put it simply: "A weak government is a negation of liberty."

Assessing the State of Democracy Through a Distorted Lens

The need for a return to Roosevelt's "Four Freedoms" as a foundation for our thought about spreading freedom in the world is evident in the annual "Freedom in the World Survey" by the congressionally funded, semiofficial U.S. organization Freedom House. These documents are revered by much of the

U.S. media and political establishment as holy writ, almost the U.S. equivalent of pronouncements by the Soviet Higher Party School. And like those pronouncements, many of Freedom House's ratings possess only a tangential relationship to reality.

What on earth, for example, are we to make of the fact that in 2006, Freedom House gave China its lowest mark, seven, for political freedom and a six for civil liberty—barely different from the seven and seven it gave in 1972, in the depth of the dreadful Cultural Revolution? Does Freedom House seriously think that ordinary Chinese are no freer today in real terms than at a time when their country was being swept by waves of monstrous totalitarian fanaticism, leading to the death, torture and deportation of tens of millions of people? Is this the same country of which two *New York Times* headlines of March 12 [2006] read, "A Sharp Debate Erupts in China Over Ideologies" and "Film in China: Fantasy trumps controversy, officially, but all movies are available one way or another." If challenged on this and similar idiocies, Freedom House officials tend to reply that they work on the basis of very narrow criteria, like free elections and private ownership of the media. But this is not an excuse—it is a confession.

Too much of the democratist ideology and its recommendations fail the test not just of study but of common sense, as well. Too many American democratists base their whole approach to the world on the assumption that they know how best to run countries of which they know nothing, whose languages they don't speak and which, quite often, they have never even visited! Would you hire a junior marketing executive with these credentials? For our part, we know perfectly well that we could not sell two plates of bean shoots in China or two sticks of kebab in Iran. We suspect, however, that most of those advocating democratism in these countries could not sell even half a plate.

> *"The America [that foreigners] see in movies and on television is often the only one they know."*

American Pop Cultural Exports Are Tarnishing the Nation's Image

Dinesh D'Souza

In the following viewpoint, Dinesh D'Souza claims that American pop culture often promotes vulgar and materialistic ideals and that these images are all that many foreign nations see of American values. D'Souza argues that this distortion is especially apparent in Islamic nations, which fear that the encroachment of American pop culture is a threat to the Muslim way of life. The fear of America's cultural exports, in D'Souza's view, explains why many Muslim resistance forces are so successful in rallying anti-American sentiment in the Arab world. He believes that Americans have to take a stand against cultural depravity at home to clean up the nation's tarnished image overseas. D'Souza was a policy analyst during the administration of President Ronald Reagan. He has since become a fellow at noted conservative public policy institutions and a successful author of several books including The Virtue of Prosperity: Finding Values in an Age of Techno Affluence.

Dinesh D'Souza, "War on Terror's Other Front: Cleaning up U.S. Pop Culture," *Christian Science Monitor*, January 25, 2007. Reproduced by permission.

As you read, consider the following questions:

1. What are some of the horrors of "blue" America that D'Souza says are repelling the Muslim world?
2. How does D'Souza interpret Osama bin Laden's assertion that Islam now faces the greatest threat it has faced since the time of Muhammad?
3. What does D'Souza think Americans should do to better the nation's cultural image?

Anti-Americanism comes in different varieties. The European kind emphasizes the "evils" of "red" America: a shoot-first, ask-questions-later cowboy in the White House, and Bible-toting fundamentalists walking around the corridors of power.

The Muslim variety is very different. Many Muslims point to the "horrors" of "blue" America: homosexual marriage, family breakdown, and a popular culture that is trivial, materialistic, vulgar, and, in many cases, morally repulsive.

This latter view is dangerously—and justifiably—common in many traditional cultures across the globe. Because it feeds their perception that American values are inimical to their way of life, this attitude can blossom into the kind of anti-American pathology that partly fueled the 9/11 attacks. Any serious effort to shore up American's security must include steps to edify American culture.

The Pop Culture Image of America Is All That Foreigners Know

Both the European and Muslim brands of anti-Americanism, of course, are focused on only one side of America. They are reacting not so much to America per se as to the often distorted projections of U.S. policy and culture across the globe. Americans know that there is a big difference between U.S. pop culture and the way they actually live. But most foreigners don't. The America they see in movies and on television is often the only one they know.

Critics of globalization complain that the United States is corrupting the world with its multinational corporations and its trade practices. But surveys such as the Pew Research Center studies of world opinion show that non-Western peoples are generally pleased with American products.

In fact, the people of Asia, Africa, and the Middle East want more American companies, more American technology, and more free trade. Their objection is not to McDonald's or Microsoft but to America's cultural values.

Arab Nations Object to Blue America

These sentiments are felt very keenly in the Muslim world. As an Iranian from Neishapour told journalist Afshin Molavi, "People say we want freedom. You know what these foreign-inspired people want? They want the freedom to gamble and drink and bring vice to our Muslim land. This is the kind of freedom they want."

Muslim critics of American culture are quick to concede its fascination and attraction, especially to the young. Some time ago, I saw an interview with a Muslim sheikh on TV. The interviewer told the sheikh, "I find it curious and hypocritical that you are so anti-American, considering that two of your sons are living and studying in America."

The sheikh replied, "But this is not hypocritical at all. I concede that American culture is appealing. If you put a young man into a hotel room and give him dozens of pornography tapes, he is likely to find those appealing as well. What America appeals to is everything that is low and disgusting in human nature."

The most powerful of all the American offenses recited in the lands of Islam, argues preeminent Middle East expert Bernard Lewis, "is the degeneracy and debauchery of the American way of life."

A major reason why some Muslims focus their anger on the United States is because it is American culture—not Swed-

Excerpt from Osama bin Laden's "Letter to America"

... We call you to be a people of manners, principles, honour, and purity; to reject the immoral acts of fornication, homosexuality, intoxicants, gambling, and trading with interest.

We call you to all of this that you may be freed from that which you have become caught up in; that you may be freed from the deceptive lies that you are a great nation, that your leaders spread amongst you to conceal from you the despicable state to which you have reached.

It is saddening to tell you that you are the worst civilization witnessed by the history of mankind: ...

You are a nation that permits acts of immorality, and you consider them to be pillars of personal freedom. You have continued to sink down this abyss from level to level until incest has spread amongst you, in the face of which neither your sense of honour nor your laws object. ...

You are a nation that exploits women like consumer products or advertising tools calling upon customers to purchase them. You use women to serve passengers, visitors, and strangers to increase your profit margins. You then rant that you support the liberation of women.

You are a nation that practices the trade of sex in all its forms, directly and indirectly. Giant corporations and establishments are established on this, under the name of art, entertainment, tourism and freedom, and other deceptive names you attribute to it.

And because of all this, you have been described in history as a nation that spreads diseases that were unknown to man in the past. Go ahead and boast to the nations of man, that you brought them AIDS as a Satanic American Invention.

Osama bin Laden, "Letter to America," November 2002.

ish culture or French culture—that is finding its way into every nook and cranny of Islamic society.

Global Resistance to American Cultural Values

There is a cultural blowback against America that is coming from all the traditional cultures of Africa, South America, the Middle East, and Asia. This resistance is summed up in a slogan used by Singapore's former prime minister, Lee Kuan Yew: "Modernization without Westernization." What this means is that traditional cultures want prosperity and technology, but they don't want the values of American culture.

The Islamic radicals are the most extreme and politically mobilized segment of this global resistance, and they are recruiting innumerable ordinary Muslims to their proclaimed jihad against the values America represents. The radicals have been remarkably successful in convincing traditional Muslims that America represents a serious threat to the Islamic religion.

In one of his post-9/11 propaganda videos, Osama bin Laden said that Islam faces the greatest threat it has faced since the time of Muhammad. How could he possibly think this? Not because of U.S. troops that were in Saudi Arabia. Not even because of Israel. The threat Bin Laden is referring to is an infiltration of American values and mores into the lives of Muslims, transforming their society and destroying their traditional values and religious beliefs.

Even the term "Great Satan," so commonly used to denounce America in the Muslim world, is better understood when we recall that in the traditional understanding, shared by Judaism, Christianity, and Islam, Satan is not a conqueror; he is a tempter. In one of its best-known verses, the Koran describes Satan as "the insidious tempter who whispers into the hearts of men."

Freedom of Expression to Some, Cultural Threat to Others

These concerns prompt a startling thought: Are the radical Muslims right? Surely, some American parents can at least sympathize. Consider the profane language on prime-time TV, or the salacious themes so prevalent in movies and music. Need I even mention the vulgarity of some rap lyrics, or the Jerry Springer and Howard Stern shows?

The Muslim indictment extends to "high culture," to liberal culture that offers itself as refined and sophisticated. In America, Eve Ensler's play, *The Vagina Monologues*, has won rave reviews and generated a pop culture phenomenon. But if its in-your-face focus on female genitalia makes some Americans uncomfortable, just imagine the reaction the performance and accompanying book is getting abroad, in places such as China, Turkey, Pakistan, and Egypt. Can foreigners be blamed for feeling defiled by this American export?

To many American liberals, pop culture reflects the values of individuality, personal autonomy, and freedom of expression. Thus, it is seen as a moral achievement. But viewed from the perspective of people in the traditional societies of the world, notably the Muslim world, these same trends appear to be nothing less than the shameless promotion of depravity.

So it is not surprising to see pious Muslims react with horror at the prospect of this new American morality seeping into their part of the world. They rightly fear that this new morality will destroy their religion and way of life.

So what should America do about this? First, it must recognize the global implications of the culture wars. Indeed the culture war and the war on terror are linked. The restoration of America's culture will be a moral boost to its children—and it will help the nation's image abroad.

As a practical matter, of course, such a cultural restoration will not be easy. At the very least, it is a task that will take decades.

Show the World America's Good Side

The best we Americans can do is to show Muslims, and traditional people around the world, the "other America" that they often don't see. Bush and his administration spokespersons should in their speeches do more to highlight the values of conservative and religious America. They should not be afraid to speak out against American cultural exports that are shameless and corrupting.

Moreover, we should do what we can to stop the export of debased American values abroad. In the United Nations, for example, America should work with Muslims, Hindus, Buddhists, and others to block the efforts of leftist groups around the world who promote radical feminism, homosexuality, prostitution, and pornography as "rights" under international law. Instead, the United States should align itself with social decency and traditional family values.

As citizens, we should not hesitate to tell traditional Muslims and others that there are many of us who are working to reverse the tide of cultural depravity in our society and around the world.

By proclaiming our allegiance to the traditional values of Judeo-Christian society, we can reduce the currents of anti-Americanism among the Muslims, and thus undercut the appeal of radical Islam to traditional Muslims around the world.

"American mass culture has not transformed the world into a replica of the United States. Instead, America's dependence on foreign cultures has made the United States a replica of the world."

American Pop Culture Exports Reflect Global Tastes

Richard Pells

Richard Pells is a professor of history at the University of Texas at Austin. In the following viewpoint, Pells describes how modern American popular culture is a reflection of the mongrel character of its people and the variety of global influences that crossed national borders since the late nineteenth century. According to Pells, American artists have liberally borrowed from other cultures in fashioning popular tastes, and the synthesis has made American culture approachable by a worldwide audience. He also argues that because much of America's art speaks to human themes, and not specifically to American values, more people around the world understand and appreciate American movies, songs, and television shows.

Richard Pells, "Is American Culture 'American?'" February 2006. http://usinfo.state.gov.

As you read, consider the following questions:

1. In Pells's view, how did European Modernism help define American popular culture?

2. Besides the effectiveness of English as a medium of cultural exchange, what are two factors that Pells says have been important in explaining American culture's popularity around the globe?

3. According to Pells, why do millions of people across the world flock to see American movies such as *Titanic*?

From the beginning of the twentieth century, people abroad have been uncomfortable with the global impact of American culture. In 1901, the British writer William Stead published a book called, ominously, *The Americanization of the World*. The title captured a set of apprehensions—about the disappearance of national languages and traditions, and the obliteration of a country's unique "identity" under the weight of American habits and states of mind—that persists until today.

More recently, globalization has been the main enemy for academics, journalists, and political activists who loathe what they see as the trend toward cultural uniformity. Still, they usually regard global culture and American culture as synonymous. And they continue to insist that Hollywood, McDonald's, and Disneyland are eradicating regional and local eccentricities—disseminating images and subliminal messages so beguiling as to drown out competing voices in other lands.

A Mongrel Culture Reflecting a Mongrel World

Despite those allegations, the cultural relationship between the United States and the rest of the world over the past 100 years has never been one-sided. On the contrary, the United States was, and continues to be, as much a consumer of foreign intellectual and artistic influences as it has been a shaper of the world's entertainment and tastes.

In fact, as a nation of immigrants from the nineteenth to the twenty-first centuries, the United States has been a recipient as much as an exporter of global culture. Indeed, the influence of immigrants on the United States explains why its culture has been so popular for so long in so many places. American culture has spread throughout the world because it has incorporated foreign styles and ideas. What Americans have done more brilliantly than their competitors overseas is repackage the cultural products we receive from abroad and then retransmit them to the rest of the planet. That is why a global mass culture has come to be identified, however simplistically, with the United States.

Americans, after all, did not invent fast food, amusement parks, or the movies. Before the Big Mac, there were fish and chips. Before Disneyland, there was Copenhagen's Tivoli Gardens (which Walt Disney used as a prototype for his first theme park in Anaheim, California, a model later re-exported to Tokyo and Paris). And in the first two decades of the twentieth century, the two largest exporters of movies around the world were France and Italy.

The Influence of Modernism

So, the origins of today's international entertainment cannot be traced only to P.T. Barnum's circuses or Buffalo Bill's Wild West Show. The roots of the new global culture lie as well in the European modernist assault, in the early twentieth century, on nineteenth-century literature, music, painting, and architectures—particularly in the modernist refusal to honor the traditional boundaries between high and low culture. Modernism in the arts was improvisational, eclectic, and irreverent. Those traits have also been characteristic of American popular culture.

The artists of the early twentieth century also challenged the notion that culture was a means of intellectual or moral improvement. They did so by emphasizing style and craftsmanship at the expense of philosophy, religion, or ideology. They deliberately called attention to language in their novels, to optics in their paintings, to the materials in and function of their architecture, to the structure of music instead of its melodies.

Although modernism was mainly a European affair, it inadvertently accelerated the growth of mass culture in the United States. Surrealism, with its dreamlike associations, easily lent itself to the wordplay and psychological symbolism of advertising, cartoons, and theme parks. Dadaism ridiculed the snobbery of elite cultural institutions and reinforced an already-existing appetite (especially among the immigrant audiences in the United States) for "low-class," disreputable nickelodeons and vaudeville shows. Stravinsky's experiments with unorthodox, atonal music validated the rhythmic innovations of American jazz.

Modernism provided the foundations for a genuinely new culture. But the new culture turned out to be neither modernist nor European. Instead, American artists transformed an avant-garde project into a global phenomenon.

Why American Entertainment Is Popular Worldwide

It is in popular culture that the reciprocal relationship between America and the rest of the world can best be seen. There are many reasons for the ascendancy of American mass culture. Certainly, the ability of American-based media conglomerates to control the production and distribution of their products has been a major stimulus for the worldwide spread of American entertainment. But the power of American capitalism is not the only, or even the most important, explanation for the global popularity of America's movies and television shows.

The effectiveness of English as a language of mass communications has been essential to the acceptance of American culture. Unlike German, Russian, or Chinese, the simpler structure and grammar of English, along with its tendency to use shorter, less abstract words and more concise sentences, are all advantageous for the composers of song lyrics, ad slogans, cartoon captions, newspaper headlines, and movie and TV dialogue. English is thus a language exceptionally well suited to the demands and spread of American mass culture.

Another factor is the international complexion of the American audience. The heterogeneity of America's population—its regional, ethnic, religious, and racial diversity—forced the media, from the early years of the twentieth century, to experiment with messages, images, and story lines that had a broad multicultural appeal. The Hollywood studios, mass-circulation magazines, and the television networks have had to learn how to speak to a variety of groups and classes at home. This has given them the techniques to appeal to an equally diverse audience abroad.

One important way that the American media have succeeded in transcending internal social divisions, national borders, and language barriers is by mixing up cultural styles. American musicians and composers have followed the example of modernist artists like Picasso and Braque in drawing on elements from high and low culture. Aaron Copland, George Gershwin, and Leonard Bernstein incorporated folk melodies, religious hymns, blues and gospel songs, and jazz into their symphonies, concertos, operas, and ballets. Indeed, an art form as quintessentially American as jazz evolved during the twentieth century into an amalgam of African, Caribbean, Latin American, and modernist European music. This blending of forms in America's mass culture has enhanced its appeal to multiethnic domestic and international audiences by capturing their different experiences and tastes.

European Influences on Hollywood

Nowhere are foreign influences more unmistakable than in the American movie industry. For better or worse, Hollywood became, in the twentieth century, the cultural capital of the modern world. But it was never an exclusively American capital. Like past cultural centers—Florence, Paris, Vienna—Hollywood has functioned as an international community, built by immigrant entrepreneurs and drawing on the talents of actors, directors, writers, cinematographers, editors, composers, and costume and set designers from all over the world.

Moreover, during much of the twentieth century, American moviemakers thought of themselves as acolytes, entranced by the superior works of foreign directors. From the 1940s to the mid-1960s, for example, Americans revered auteurs like Ingmar Bergman, Federico Fellini, Michelangelo Antonioni, François Truffaut, Jean-Luc Godard, Akira Kurosawa, and Satyajit Ray.

Nevertheless, it is one of the paradoxes of the European and Asian cinema that its greatest success was in spawning American imitations. By the 1970s, the newest geniuses— Francis Ford Coppola, Martin Scorsese, Robert Altman, Steven Spielberg, Woody Allen—were American. The Americans owed their improvisational methods and autobiographical preoccupations to Italian neo-Realism and the French New Wave. But the use of these techniques revolutionized the American cinema, making it even harder for any other continent's film industry to match the worldwide popularity of American movies.

Still, American directors in every era have emulated foreign artists and filmmakers by paying close attention to the style and formal qualities of a movie, and to the need to tell a story visually. Early twentieth-century European painters wanted viewers to recognize that they were looking at lines and color on a canvas rather than at a reproduction of the natural world. Similarly, many American films—from the multiple narrators in *Citizen Kane*, to the split-screen portrait of how two lovers imagine their relationship in *Annie Hall*, to the flashbacks and flash-forwards in *Pulp Fiction*—deliberately remind the audience that it is watching a movie instead of a

American Slang Is a Badge of Belonging to a Global Youth Culture

Vernacular English is powerfully expressive because—paradoxically—it is both exclusive and global. In any host society, American slang lives in a world of linguistic and cultural knowledge not available at school or in mainstream media. (This also holds true for Jamaican English slang which is popular among fans of reggae and dancehall music.) American slang lives in the specialized media of the young, such as CD booklets, songs and video clips, magazines and Web sites. Through the media, young people enter fan communities where they learn to incorporate certain forms of English into both their speech and writing to show that they're a part of youth culture. As a result, American slang and related resources have become a global code for youth worldwide embedded in a local code—the national language.

Jannis Androutsopoulos,
"Do You Speak American?" 2002. www.pbs.org.

photographed version of reality. American filmmakers (not only in the movies but on MTV) have been willing to use the most sophisticated techniques of editing and camera work, much of it inspired by foreign directors, to create a modernist collage of images that captures the speed and seductiveness of life in the contemporary world.

Speaking to Human, Not American, Traits

Hollywood's addiction to modernist visual pyrotechnics is especially evident in the largely nonverbal style of many of its contemporary performers. After Marlon Brando's revolutionary performance in *A Streetcar Named Desire*, on stage in 1947 and in the 1951 screen version, the model of American acting became inarticulateness—a brooding introspection that one doesn't find in the glib and fast-talking heroes or heroines of the screwball comedies and gangster films of the 1930s.

Brando was trained in the Method, an acting technique originally developed in Stanislavsky's Moscow Art Theater in pre-Revolutionary Russia. The Method encouraged actors to improvise, to summon up childhood memories and inner feelings, often at the expense of what a playwright or screen-writer intended. Thus, the emotional power of American act-ing—as exemplified by Brando and his successors—often lay more in what was not said, in the exploration of passions that could not be communicated in words.

The influence of the Method, not only in the United States but also abroad where it was reflected in the acting styles of Jean-Paul Belmondo and Marcello Mastroianni, is a classic ex-ample of how a foreign idea, originally meant for the stage, was adapted in postwar America to the movies, and then con-veyed to the rest of the world as a paradigm for both cin-ematic and social behavior. More important, the Method actor's disregard for language, the reliance on physical man-nerisms and even on silence in interpreting a role, has permit-ted global audiences—even those not well-versed in En-glish—to understand and appreciate what they are watching in American films.

Focusing on Human Relationships

Finally, American culture has imitated not only the modernists' visual flamboyance, but also their tendency to be apolitical and anti-ideological. The refusal to browbeat an audience with a social message has accounted, more than any other factor, for the worldwide popularity of American entertainment. American movies, in particular, have customarily focused on human relationships and private feelings, not on the problems of a particular time and place. They tell tales about romance, intrigue, success, failure, moral conflicts, and survival. The most memorable movies of the 1930s (with the exception of *The Grapes of Wrath*) were comedies and musicals about mismatched people falling in love, not socially conscious films dealing with issues of poverty and unemployment. Similarly, the finest movies about World War II (like *Casablanca*) or the Vietnam War (like *The Deer Hunter*) linger in the mind long after those conflicts have ended because they explore their characters' most intimate emotions rather than dwelling on headline events.

Such intensely personal dilemmas are what people everywhere wrestle with. So Europeans, Asians, and Latin Americans flocked to *Titanic*, as they once did to *Gone With the Wind*, not because those films celebrated American values, but because people all over the world could see some part of their own lives reflected in the stories of love and loss.

America's mass culture has often been crude and intrusive, as its critics have always complained. But American culture has never felt all that foreign to foreigners. And, at its best, it has transformed what it received from others into a culture everyone, everywhere, could embrace—a culture that is both emotionally and, on occasion, artistically compelling for millions of people throughout the world.

So, despite the current resurgence of anti-Americanism—not only in the Middle East but in Europe and Latin America—it is important to recognize that America's movies, television shows, and theme parks have been less "imperialistic" than cosmopolitan. In the end, American mass culture has not transformed the world into a replica of the United States. Instead, America's dependence on foreign cultures has made the United States a replica of the world.

Periodical Bibliography

The following articles have been selected to supplement the diverse views presented in this chapter.

Derek Chollet and Tod Lindberg	"A Moral Core for U.S. Foreign Policy," *Policy Review*, December 2007–January 2008.
Amitai Etzioni	"Will the Right Islam Stand Up?" *Sociological Forum*, March 2008.
Joshua Kurlantzick	"The Decline of American Soft Power," *Current History*, December 2005.
Scott McCartney	"Teaching Americans How to Behave Abroad," *The Wall Street Journal*, April 11, 2006.
Joseph S. Nye Jr.	"The Smarter Superpower," *Foreign Policy*, May-June 2007.
George Cardinal Pell	"Islam and Us," *First Things: A Monthly Journal of Religion & Public Life*, June-July 2006.
Ziauddin Sardar	"A Common Heritage for Global Peace," *New Statesman*, December 10, 2007.
John Shattuck	"Healing Our Self-Inflicted Wounds," *American Prospect*, January-February 2008.
David W. Shenk	"The Gospel of Reconciliation Within the Wrath of Nations," *International Bulletin of Missionary Research*, January 2008.
Paul Starobin	"Misfit America," *Atlantic Monthly*, January-February 2006.
Mark Steyn	"Don't Worry, They Have Baseball Bats," *National Review*, December 5, 2005.
Jordan Stuart	"How We Can Win the Global Culture War," *Free Inquiry*, February-March 2006.
Manfred Weidhorn	"Islam's Presumed Superiority to the West," *Midwest Quarterly*, Autumn 2007.

For Further Discussion

Chapter 1

1. In his viewpoint, Mitt Romney states, "Freedom requires religion just as religion requires freedom. Freedom opens the windows of the soul so that man can discover his most profound beliefs and commune with God. Freedom and religion endure together, or perish alone." Explain what Romney means by this assertion. Then, declare whether you agree or disagree with the statement. When framing your answer, be sure to address Ira Chernus's opinions about what he perceives as the political abuses of religion in America.

2. How do Bob Ditmar and Jason Miller utilize historical trends and events to support their contrasting views about the supposed virtue of American capitalism? What other types of arguments do both use to bolster their claims?

3. Andrei Cherny and Stan Moore share the opinion that American democracy has been abused by powerful elites in modern times. However, Cherny has a rather optimistic opinion that Americans can reinvigorate democracy, while Moore expresses a more pessimistic view of the future of U.S.-style democracy both at home and overseas. Explain what informs each author's vision of democracy. Then, decide whether your own views of democracy in America are optimistic or pessimistic.

Chapter 2

1. Jacob Hornberger argues the libertarian view that government robs Americans of their freedom because it demands their money to support a welfare state. Hornberger, in essence, equates personal liberty with economic liberty. Wil-

liam A. Galston, however, contends that many welfare programs have virtually eliminated real social problems such as poverty among the elderly (Social Security) and therefore should not be disparaged because they limit individual freedom for the sake of the entire community. Galston believes that freedom is not solely defined by personal choice. Whose view do you find more convincing? Explain your answer by citing arguments from the two viewpoints.

2. After reading the final three viewpoints in this chapter, explain how you think America's value for money (and its attendant ideas of thrift and consumerism) have changed over the past several decades. Ted Nugent, Ray Boshara, and Phillip Longman advocate a return to lost ideals of hard work and saving. Do you believe that these ideals no longer exist? Explain why or why not. In answering the question, be sure to describe the ideals that you think dominate Americans' use of money today.

Chapter 3

1. Ben Shapiro argues that American nationalism is a force of good in the world because it promotes democracy and other positive American values. He asserts that America's form of nationalism is constructed with "the highest set of values ever embodied in national form." Howard Zinn maintains that America has sought to impose its values on other nations by force. He believes that it is dangerous for America to think of itself as superior to other nations. Do you believe that America's nationalist spirit and its drive to spread its values are forces of good or potentially hazardous foreign policies? Explain your answer.

2. How does Jonathan M. Hansen defend liberal dissent in America during the war on terror? Why does Aryeh Spero

reject this view of liberal patriotism? Citing arguments from both viewpoints, explain whose view you find more compelling.

Chapter 4

1. After reading the viewpoints by David Blankenhorn and Dean Robinson, explain whether you think a dialogue between Christian and Islamic scholars would be an effective means of bridging the gap between the West and the Arab world? In answering the question, consider Robinson's assertion that Islam is not only a faith, but also an important part of political and economic policy in Muslim nations.

2. Anatol Lieven and John Hulsman claim that American attempts to export democracy are often perceived as another aspect of U.S. imperialism. Under what circumstances do these authors believe that democracy might take hold in the Arab world? After reading Richard Warren Field's viewpoint, decide what role America could play in helping to bring about these requisite circumstances?

3. In considering the arguments of Dinesh D'Souza and Richard Pells, enumerate both the positive and negative messages conveyed through American pop culture exports (film, music, music videos, fashion, etc.). Then, explain whether you think America should take action to tame or bolster the image it presents to the outside world.

Organizations to Contact

The editors have compiled the following list of organizations concerned with the issues debated in this book. The descriptions are derived from materials provided by the organizations. All have publications or information available for interested readers. The list was compiled on the date of publication of the present volume; the information provided here may change. Be aware that many organizations take several weeks or longer to respond to inquiries, so allow as much time as possible.

American Civil Liberties Union (ACLU)
125 Broad Street, 18th Floor, New York, NY 10004
(212) 607-3300 • fax: (212) 607-3318
Web site: www.aclu.org

The American Civil Liberties Union (ACLU) works through its affiliates in every state of the union to protect the values and freedoms guaranteed to all Americans by the Bill of Rights in the Constitution. Specifically, the ACLU works to preserve First Amendment rights, equal protection under the law, the right to due process, individuals' right to privacy, and the rights of minority individuals such as people of color, homosexuals, women, and people with disabilities. The ACLU offers e-mail subscriptions to receive regular newsletters from the organization with up-to-date information on civil liberties related happenings and actions individuals can take to stay involved. Additionally, other annual reports and press releases can be searched and viewed on the organization's Web site.

American Enterprise Institute (AEI)
1150 Seventeenth Street NW, Washington, DC 20036
(202) 862-5800 • fax: (202) 862-7177
Web site: www.aei.org

The American Enterprise Institute (AEI) provides research and educational materials concerning social, political, and economic issues in the United States. Experts from various fields including law, ethics, theology, and political science contribute to the institute's research, conferences, and publications. Ideals such as limited government, private enterprise, individual liberty, vigilant defense and foreign policy, and open debate form the basis for AEI's work. *The American* is the bimonthly magazine of the institute; articles from this publication and others are accessible online.

American Family Association (AFA)

PO Drawer 2440, Tupelo, MS 38803
(662) 844-5036 • fax: (662) 842-7798
Web site: www.afa.net

Founded in 1977, the American Family Association (AFA) is a Christian organization dedicated to fighting the forces responsible for the decline of traditional family values. The association sees television and other media as the greatest culprit in promoting negative values through portrayals of violence, premarital sex, and other detriments. AFA sends a monthly letter to its supporters suggesting a cause worthy of their involvement. Additionally, the *AFA Journal* provides news on issues such as the negative impacts of gambling, the importance of fighting same-sex marriage, and ways to protect children and teens from the negative influence of the media.

American Values

PO Box 96192, Washington, DC 20090-619
(703) 671-9700 • fax: (703) 671-1680
Web site: www.amvalues.org

American Values is a nonprofit organization that supports conservative values to maintain a "nation that embraces life, marriage, family, faith, and freedom." It stands against liberal media and its eroding influence on traditional views of marriage, family, and education. The organization's Web site offers position statements on pro-life, pro-family issues.

Cato Institute
1000 Massachusetts Avenue NW, Washington, DC 20001
(202) 842-0200 • fax: (202) 842-3490
Web site: www.cato.org

Founded in 1977, the Cato Institute seeks to advance government policies associated with libertarian values such as limited government, individual liberty, free markets, and peace, all of which Cato views as fundamental American values upon which the country was founded. The organization publishes numerous books, reports, and studies addressing all aspects of American society and values such as bioethics, education, law and civil liberties, and political philosophy. Cato's Web site provides electronic copies of many of these reports.

Common Dreams
PO Box 443, Portland, ME 04112
(207) 775-0488 • fax: (207) 775-0489
e-mail: editor@commondreams.org
Web site: www.commondreams.org

Common Dreams is a nonprofit, citizens' organization dedicated to promoting progressive ideas and policies for the future of America. To this end, the organization's Web site provides current news stories from and about activists that are often filtered out of the mainstream media. Up-to-date articles, as well as archived collections of articles, are available at the site.

Democratic National Committee (DNC)
430 S. Capitol Street SE, Washington, DC 20003
(202) 863-8000
Web site: www.democrats.org

Founded in 1792 by Thomas Jefferson to oppose the elitist Federalist Party, the Democratic Party works to promote the principles of strength, inclusion, and opportunity, which it sees as the ideals upon which America was founded. Further, the Democratic Party advocates for the maintenance of a welfare state in which those who are least capable of supporting themselves receive assistance from the collective state. The Web site of the Democratic National Committee (DNC) offers articles outlining the agenda of the party as well as press releases and news updates on specific actions being taken to pursue party goals.

Focus on the Family
Colorado Springs, CO 80995
(800) 232-6459
Web site: www.family.org

Focus on the Family preaches the importance of both the Christian faith and family values to societies and communities worldwide. The guiding principles promoted by the organization are the preeminence of evangelism, permanence of marriage, the value of children, the sanctity of human life, and the importance of social responsibility. The Focus on the Family Web site provides articles and guides on topics such as marriage, bioethics, education, and sexual identity. *Citizen* is the monthly magazine of the organization.

Heritage Foundation
214 Massachusetts Avenue NE, Washington, DC 20002
(202) 546-4400 • fax: (202) 546-8328
e-mail: info@heritage.org
Web site: www.heritage.org

The Heritage Foundation, a conservative public-policy organization, works to establish and promote policies that align with the principles of free enterprise, limited government, individual freedom, traditional American values, and a strong national defense. As such, the organization advocates for policies that allow choice in education, health care, and retirement; support individuals to achieve as much as possible based on their talents; and encourage reduced government involvement in the lives of Americans. Reports and policy papers on issues such as education, family and marriage, and sex education and abstinence are all available on the Heritage Foundation's Web site.

Institute for American Values

1841 Broadway, Suite 211, New York, NY 10023
(212) 246-3942 • fax: (212) 541-6665
e-mail: info@americanvalues.org
Web site: www.americanvalues.org

The Institute for American Values was founded in 1987 to promote government policies that support the development of strong family units and civil societies on a national and global level. The organization works to provide information to policy makers, the media, and the public in general through its Malta Forum, the council on Family Law, and various academic and professional advisory committees. The institute has published books such as *Between Two Worlds: The Inner Lives of Children of Divorce, The Islam/West Debate: Documents from a Global Debate on Terrorism, U.S. Policy and the Middle East,* and *Why Marriage Matters: Twenty-Six Conclusions from the Social Sciences.* Additionally, other reports and commentaries on value-related issues are available on the organization's Web site.

Libertarian Party

2600 Virginia Avenue NW, Suite 200, Washington, DC 20037
(800) 353-2887
Web site: www.lp.org

Founded in 1971, the Libertarian Party promotes the idea of limited government interference in both economic and social aspects of life. As such, the party advocates for lower taxes and charitable, not government, welfare as well as an absence of laws dictating how individuals must live their lives, as long as these lifestyles do not harm other citizens. A copy of the Libertarian Party's National Platform as well as position papers on current issues are accessible on the Party's Web site.

People for the American Way (PFAW)

2000 M Street NW, Suite 400, Washington, DC 20036
(202) 467-4999
e-mail: pfaw@pfaw.org
Web site: www.pfaw.org

People for the American Way (PFAW) advocates government policies and ideals that preserve the diversity that is characteristic of American, democratic society. The organization maintains that conservative power structures erode the fundamental rights and freedom guaranteed by the Constitution. To protect and promote the values it sees central to the American way of life, PFAW publishes educational materials for the public on topics such as civil and equal rights, religious freedom, and public education, and has also founded projects such as the Center for American Values in Public Life. Individuals can subscribe to electronic newsletters and updated press releases on the organization's Web site.

Republican National Committee (RNC)
310 First Street, Washington, DC   20003
(202) 863-8500 • fax: (202) 863-8820
e-mail: info@gop.com
Web site: www.gop.com

Founded officially in 1854 by antislavery activists and settlers who advocated for the right to take western lands without charge, the Republican Party's cornerstone principles included limited government, government exercise of fiscal responsibility, and recognition of individual ability. Accordingly, the Grand Old Party (GOP) does not support the idea of a welfare state, maintaining that instead of providing direct assistance to citizens, the government must only ensure that every person has the opportunity to create a sustainable life. Republicans see free enterprise and encouragement of individual initiative as the best methods for ensuring growth and prosperity. Position statements and current news on party issues are available on the Republic National Committee's (RNC) Web site.

Bibliography of Books

Peter Applebome   *Dixie Rising: How the South Is Shaping American Values, Politics, and
Culture.* New York: Times Books,
1996.

Wayne E. Baker   *America's Crisis of Values: Reality and
Perception.* Princeton, NJ: Princeton
University Press, 2006.

Michael Billig   *Banal Nationalism.* Thousand Oaks,
CA: Sage, 1995.

Doris Buss and   *Globalizing Family Values: The Chris-
Didi Herman   tian Right in International Politics.*
Minneapolis: University of Minnesota
Press, 2003.

William M. Fox   *American Values Decline: What We
Can Do.* Bloomington, IN: 1st Books,
2001.

Newt Gingrich   *Rediscovering God in America: Reflec-
tions on the Role of Faith in Our
Nation's History.* Nashville, TN: Thomas Nelson, 2006.

Norval D. Glenn   *With This Ring. . .: A National Survey
on Marriage in America.* Gaithers-
burg, MD: National Fatherhood Initiative, 2005.

Glenn Greenwald   *How Would a Patriot Act? Defending
American Values from a President Run
Amok.* San Francisco, CA: Working
Assets, 2006.

William E.
Hudson
American Democracy in Peril: Eight Challenges to America's Future. Washington, DC: CQ Press, 2006.

James Davison
Hunter and
Alan Wolfe
Is There a Culture War?: A Dialogue on Values and American Public Life. Washington, DC: Brookings Institution, 2006.

Josef Joffe
Überpower: The Imperial Temptation of America. New York: Norton, 2006.

Eun Y. Kim
The Yin and Yang of American Culture: A Paradox. Boston, MA: Intercultural, 2001.

Anatol Lieven
America Right or Wrong: An Anatomy of American Nationalism. New York: Oxford University Press, 2005.

Brink Lindsey
The Age of Abundance: How Prosperity Transformed America's Politics and Culture. New York: Collins, 2007.

Robert S.
McElvaine
Grand Theft Jesus: The Hijacking of Religion in America. New York: Crown, 2008.

George McKenna
The Puritan Origins of American Patriotism. New Haven, CT: Yale University Press, 2007.

Michael Nazir-Ali
Conviction and Conflict: Islam, Christianity and World Order. London: Continuum, 2006.

Keith Olbermann — *Truth and Consequences: Special Comments on the Bush Administration's War on American Values*. New York: Random House, 2007.

Stephen Prothero, ed. — *A Nation of Religions: The Politics of Pluralism in Multireligious America*. Chapel Hill: University of North Carolina Press, 2006.

B. Wayne Quist and David F. Drake — *Winning the War on Terror: A Triumph of American Values*. Bloomington, IN: iUniverse, 2005.

Jeffrey Stout — *Democracy and Tradition*. Princeton, NJ: Princeton University Press, 2005.

Steven M. Tipton and John Witte Jr. — *Family Transformed: Religion, Values, and Society in American Life*. Washington, DC: Georgetown University Press, 2005.

John Kenneth White — *Values Divide: American Politics and Culture in Transition*. New York: Chatham House, 2002.

Harvey S. Wiener and Nora Eisenberg, eds. — *The American Values Reader*. Boston, MA: Allyn & Bacon, 1999.

Alan Wolfe — *One Nation, After All: What Americans Really Think About God, Country, Family, Racism, Welfare, Immigration, Homosexuality, Work, the Right, the Left and Each Other*. New York: Penguin, 1999.

Index